52 brilliantideas
one good idea can change your life...

wish you were logorrhoea.

Inspired
creative writing
Secrets of the master wordsmiths

Alexander Gordon Smith

Copyright © The Infinite Ideas Company Limited, 2005

The right of Alexander Gordon Smith to be identified as the author of this
book has been asserted in accordance with the Copyright, Designs and Patents
Act 1988

First published in 2004 by
The Infinite Ideas Company Limited
Belsyre Court
57 Woodstock Road
Oxford
OX2 6HJ
United Kingdom
www.infideas.com

CIP catalogue records for this book are available from the British Library and
the US Library of Congress.

ISBN 1-904902-07-3

Brand and product names are trademarks or registered trademarks of their
respective owners.

Designed and typeset by Baseline Arts Ltd, Oxford
Printed and bound by TJ International, Cornwall

Inspired creative writing

Brilliant ideas

Brilliant features xiii

Introduction xiv

1. **Limbering up** 1
   Looking down at that blank page can send tsunami-sized shivers down your spine, but
   don't give in to the temptation to run for cover screaming, victory is just a scribble away.

2. **Taking the plunge** 5
   You may think your muse has passed you by, but it might be that she's the kind of girl
   who whispers rather than shouts. Ideas are everywhere, you just need to learn how to
   spot them.

3. **Second sight** 11
   We're all wearing blinkers, and like a plough-horse finally lifting its head to see the
   mountains, we've got to learn that there's more around us than mud. It's time to find
   our second sight.

4. **Playing games** 15
   Down at the English faculty, creative writing is a serious business for serious people.
   But writers don't want to work all of the time. Some simple game play can be fun and
   inspirational.

5. **Shall I compare thee to a summer's day?**...19
   How do you stop the big things from having little meaning and the little things from
   getting too big and messy? Confused? Me too.

6. **Blowing your trumpet** 25

If you're like me, some days you probably think there isn't much floating around in the memory department of your brain except for a few old episodes of Thundercats. But learn to dive in deeper – your past can be the key to great writing.

7. **Digging the dirt**...29

Research. It's for academics and non-fiction writers, right? Wrong. Your imagination is what drives a piece of writing, but you really need to do your homework if you want to look convincing.

8. **When the rhythm starts to play**...33

Life is full of natural rhythms – just try walking to an irregular beat, you'll be falling over yourself in no time. You don't have to write sonnets to get rhythm into your poetry, just keep your ears open to nature's pulse.

9. **There once was a man from Kentuckett...**...37

When I started writing poetry, I never knew how to shape it on the page. I could never decide where to break the bloody lines and so it always ended up as prose. Thankfully, finding the right form for self-expression is easier than you think.

10. **Style is everything!** 43

The style you choose to write in can say an awful lot about you. Don't be shy and don't be false, just act natural: like your sense of dress, your writing style should be personal and unique to you.

11 **A sensuous, transcendent, sublime chapter** 47

Language is a powerful device. You can use it to create any thing or any mood you want. Ensuring that every word is efficiently placed and full of meaning is the first step towards writing that really packs a punch.

12 **That's so abstract, dude** 51

Writing is about exploring the parts of yourself you don't really understand; grappling with what it means to be human. To do this, you need a more powerful arsenal to work with than a few abstract terms.

13 **Who's the daddy: character or plot?** 55

Like it or not, it's your characters that drive your work. Getting them right will make the difference between writing a masterpiece and an episode of Days of Our Lives.

14 **Born slippy** 59

Creating realistic characters is as much a case of looking inwards as it is looking outwards. Learn to see what really makes people unique, mix these characteristics up and just wait for the newborns to emerge.

15 **You are what you own** 65

Whether it's a tattered sombrero, a life-size Elvis doll or a 1970s Jaguar, what your characters own says everything about them. These tricks will help you bring them to life.

16 **Say what?** 69

There's little worse than characters that don't speak proper – believable dialogue is the first step to a believable world, and is a great way to get to know who your characters really are...

17 **Accent marks** 73

You may have the most realistically depicted characters in literary history, but if they fall to pieces as soon as they open their mouth then nobody is going to take them seriously. Fear not, your voice coach has arrived...

18 **There may be trouble ahead** 77

The most memorable fictional characters all face up to some kind of conflict – from global threats to personal dilemmas – so learn to treat 'em mean if you want to keep the readers keen.

19 **It's alive!**...83

So, you know your characters inside out, you can picture them in your head, you can smell their perfume, and you know exactly what drives them to act. Now you just have to convey all of this on the page...

20 **Fast and furious**..87

Film characters are only on screen for a couple of hours, so they have to move fast. Use these tried and tested methods for getting the audience on your side as soon as the curtains open.

21 **Playing god**...91

Every piece of writing has to have a viewpoint. Somebody, or something, has to tell the story, and the choice has profound implications for the way a reader engages with your text.

22 **Variations on a theme**..95

Just because you want to use a third-person narrator in your writing doesn't mean he/she/it has to be omniscient. The third-person limited could be just the compromise you're looking for.

23 **What are you looking at?**..99

It's rare, but when used effectively second-person narration can knock the reader's socks off.

24 **Through the eyes of the beholder**...105

If you're looking for an intense and surprising narrative viewpoint, try the first person. Anybody or anything you like can be telling the story – the trick is to avoid 'I' becoming 'you'...

25 **Too many cooks**...109

A piece of fiction can come to resemble the Black Hole of Calcutta – sweaty, noisy and horrible to be in. Learn to avoid this by restraining your cast.

26 **It's all in the past**..113
Or is it? Here's how to select the right tense for your fiction, and some ideas to help
you decide whether or not to obey the rules.

27 **Changing lanes**..117
Your narrative style should steer readers – we're talking a gentle hand on the arm, not
a guide dog. Sometimes, though, it can be exciting to let go and give the reader a real
wake-up call.

28 **Virtual realty**...123
So, you've recruited your characters, you know them intimately and even have an inkling
of where they're heading...but don't get so carried away with the drama that you forget
about the setting in which it unfolds.

29 **Changing rooms**..127
Everywhere, no matter how mundane, has an atmosphere. Learn to tune into this in order
to create a three-dimensional, multi-sensory world.

30 **Keeping up with the Joneses**..131
A person's surroundings are more than just wrapping paper. The places people go and
the objects they interact with can reveal more about them than they like to think – use
this hidden language for powerful characterisation.

31 **There's no place like home**...135
Look around you at the place you live, really look around. Familiarity may have made it
seem a little dull, but this is your world, and it's too valuable a resource to ignore.

32 **Poetic licence**..141
Novels, stories and screenplays aren't the only things that need a setting. Poetry also relies
on the visual to convey a sense of mood and meaning. But when writing a poem, a great
deal more depends on how you choose to decorate.

33 **Westerns, waterworlds and beavers** 145
It's vital that you pin down the theme of whatever you're writing. Why? Because the theme is the heart of a piece of writing, it's the very blood that flows through it.

34 **Every which way but loose** 149
You've created your characters. Now it's time for them to do something. Get to grips with plot – the sequence of related events that's the most interesting and dramatically effective way of telling the story.

35 **Who's got the map?** 153
Whether your plot is driving your work or following in the wake of your characters there are certain techniques to getting from A to B without losing your passengers. Try the classical approach...

36 **All good things come in threes** 159
Tackling the intricacies of script plotting in a single chapter is like trying to squeeze Arnold Schwarzenegger into a romper suit. But try these useful pointers to keep things moving in the right direction.

37 **Buy one, get everything else free** 163
Having a clear idea of where your work is heading is all well and good, but remember: readers don't like a giveaway, so keep them guessing by plotting cleverly.

38 **Coming over all emotional** 167
How can you, the screenwriter, make sure your audience gets emotionally involved with on-screen events? Hooking viewers is like catching fish – you've just got to find the right bait.

39 **Subletting your story** 171
Subplots may seem like unnecessary baggage, but they're vital to creating a believable and engaging story.

40 **Yakety yak, don't talk back**..177

Ah, we get to it at last, the great debate. Rhyme. Sometimes it's in, sometimes it's just so passé; some people consider it compulsory, others unnecessary. Let's look at the reasons for rhyme.

41 **Size doesn't matter**...181

Short stories take a moment in time selected from a much larger narrative, compress characters and meaning into a tiny space and (hopefully) create something intense and beautiful.

42 **Show and tell** 185

The first commandment of writing: show, don't tell. By showing you're letting the reader project something of their own experience into the writing. Showing is sharing – always the nice thing to do.

43 **The big read**..189

It will be hard, it may even be nasty, but you have to re-read your work in order to improve it. Get your 'built in shit-detector' ready.

44 **Armageddon** 195

People either avoid editing altogether or try and squeeze it in at the most inopportune moment – when writing. To get the most from your internal editor, stop it barging in and ask it to make an appointment.

45 **Surgery or butchery?** 199

You'd be surprised how much even the smallest nip and tuck will improve your finished work. Keep your mind open to revision.

46 **Getting down and dirty** 203

Workshops and writers' groups aren't the terrifying interrogations that the uninitiated often make them out to be. Joining up could be the best thing you've ever done.

47 **Spring cleaning**..209
You wouldn't visit your publisher wearing dirty rags – so don't send them a manuscript
that looks like it's just come out of your dog's rear end.

48 **Learn to let go**..213
The big day has finally arrived. You can't do anything else to your novel – it's perfect.
So stop staring at it and get it out there. The world wants to know your name.

49 **Don't cause a drama**...217
Your first script is finished. Great! What are you waiting for? You should whack it straight
out to an agent, right? Hold your horses. It's a war out there. Make sure you've got
reinforcements.

50 **The short and curlies**..223
It may be tempting to start sending boxfuls of your poetry and short stories to as many
magazines as you can find. But hold up – there are techniques to getting your short work
published.

51 **The good, the bad and the ugly**..227
Submitting your work is like dropping your kids off for their first day at school. You don't
know whether they are going to be bullied, rejected or become best friends with everybody
and make a real impression. Be prepared for all eventualities.

52 **It's all about you...**..231
If you remember only one thing, make sure it's this: what makes your writing powerful
and unique is you, so always learn to trust your instincts.

The End 236
Or is it a new beginning?

Where it's at 238
Index

Brilliant features

Each chapter of this book is designed to provide you with an inspirational idea that you can read quickly and put into practice straight away.

Throughout you'll find four features that will help you to get right to the heart of the idea:

- *Try another idea* If this idea looks like a life-changer then there's no time to lose. *Try another idea* will point you straight to a related tip to expand and enhance the first.

- *Here's an idea for you* Give it a go – right here, right now – and get an idea of how well you're doing so far.

- *Defining ideas* Words of wisdom from masters and mistresses of the art, plus some interesting hangers-on.

- *How did it go?* If at first you do succeed try to hide your amazement. If, on the other hand, you don't this is where you'll find a Q and A that highlights common problems and how to get over them.

Introduction

*'If the doctor told me I had six minutes to live,
I'd type a little faster.'*
ISAAC ASIMOV

**When I first started to write fiction I came across
a quote by W. Somerset Maugham that began 'there are three rules
to writing a novel'. Great, I thought, this should be easy! Three
rules, I can cope with that. Imagine my disappointment when the
quote went on to say 'unfortunately, no one knows what they are'.**

It's one of life's great truisms: there are no rules to writing creatively. It's not like
putting up a flat-pack wardrobe or learning to work your microwave. The sheer
number of quotes I've come across in the last few months says it all: everybody does
things their own way, and everybody gives different advice.

But I guess that's what lies at the heart of creative writing, that's what makes it such
a powerful means of expression. If there were set rules to follow, we'd all be doing
it, we'd all be millionaires, bookshops would be as big as countries and nothing
would be worth reading. The fact is that all good writing comes from the heart, it's
unique to the person who wrote it, it's a piece of them unleashed onto the paper,
something nobody else could have written. This absence of rules is what makes
writing so personal, so evocative and so magical.

This isn't a rulebook. It's a collection of the hints, exercises and priceless nuggets of information I've picked up over the years as a writer, editor and publisher. Some of this is centred around the technical details, most is focused on ways to help you free your creative side, to conquer your fears and enable you to write something you'll always be proud of, and which will hopefully end up in print.

Writing is about so much more than plot, character, setting, rhythm, style, rhyme and so on. But finding ways to express yourself successfully and creatively means learning the basics first. I hope the ideas in this book will give you a good understanding of the process of writing, but more than that I hope it inspires you, gives you that burning, insatiable passion to write. If it doesn't, I haven't done the craft justice.

Lastly, I'm one of those people who buys *Men's Health* every month thinking that reading it will give me a six-pack. Don't take this approach with your writing. This book will give you some excellent advice on how to explore your creative depths and write convincingly on the page, but reading it from cover to cover won't make you the next Booker winner. If you want to be successful, there's only one way. You have to write, write, write. Good luck!

'I am not a writer except when I write.'
JUAN CARLOS ONETTI

1

Limbering up

Looking down at that blank page can send tsunami-sized shivers down your spine, but don't give in to the temptation to run for cover screaming, victory is just a scribble away.

The blank page is a monster, far worse than any Hollywood nightmare.

The blank page wages a war of fear and ridicule. It taunts you, it tells you it will never be filled, that anything you write will be a mere shadow of what's gone before. But be brave, take the plunge, and remember that this villain can be vanquished with a simple stroke of your pen.

FIRST STEPS

A common mistake when facing up to this immense white expanse is to believe that you can decorate it with a masterpiece straight away. The blank page wants you to think like this, as it's the first step to obliterating your confidence and self-respect. If you try to go for the big one first time, if you think you can wipe the smug expression from that blank with an instant work of sheer genius, then chances are after a few lines you will surrender and spend your days as a remorseful prisoner of war.

Here's an idea for you...

Do this every day. Take a blank sheet of paper, and just write for a set time at a set time. With each passing day your sketches should become more solid and less hesitant, as your confidence builds. Pick random subjects to write about and make sure you include the details, however small. When you feel up to it, start to put the bits and pieces you have been writing into a short story or a poem. You should find that the details you thought were unnecessary enable you to paint a vivid picture of something you've always taken for granted.

A LITTLE AT A TIME

Most successful writers will tell you that a conflict with the blank page must be a war of attrition, not a full-on nuclear strike. The only path to victory is to gradually convert that white expanse into a page of words, your words. They don't have to be a masterpiece. In fact, they don't even have to be a story, or a poem, or a screenplay, they just have to make sense to you. Begin with random words and convert them into sentences – let them lead you. Before you know it, the blank page has shrunk, its taunts are fainter, mere whispers, and then it's gone. Don't think about what you're writing – nobody but you is ever going to see it – just keep that pen moving or those keys tapping until your old adversary has vanished. Those stuttered fragments will become paragraphs, then pages, and after a while you'll wonder why on earth that innocuous white sheet of processed wood was giving you the cold sweats.

GET OFF RUNNING

OK, it's easy for me to say 'just write', but if you are still sitting facing the first page of your notepad or that virgin screen, then it may not seem so simple. The first thing to do is to get rid of the idea that you are about to start writing a finished piece. Don't try and carve out a first line of absolute genius, or write the beginnings of an epic tale you've had in your head for years, as you'll be putting yourself under an unhealthy amount of pressure. Instead, start writing a few words about the last relative that visited, your most memorable holiday, the state of your neighbour's garden, the last great argument you had.

Take practically any topic you like – if your mind is still blank, make a note of any sounds you can hear or sights from your window, or just open a dictionary at a random page and pick the first recognisable word. And once you've got that subject just start writing. Don't stop, don't edit, just gear yourself towards writing as much as possible in four or five minutes. Once you've started charging forwards, you'll find the words come more and more easily.

It's all very well jotting down scraps, but how do you get those 'Eureka' ideas? IDEA 2, *Taking the plunge*, gives a few clues.

Try another idea...

'Writing is easy; all you have to do is sit staring at a blank sheet of paper until the drops of blood form on your forehead.'
GENE FOWLER, writer and director

Defining idea...

How did it go?

Q   I can beat the blank page monster sometimes but on other days I dive behind the sofa quivering. Any suggestions, other than therapy?

A   *Writing practice needs discipline. Like Virginia Woolf, who could only write in the morning, you need to find a time of day that you usually have free and make yourself write. That's right, make yourself. Even if you don't want to, write for a few minutes. Before long, you should settle into a routine and begin to really make the most of your writing time. If you find it difficult to get started again day after day, then cheat – leave out the last paragraph of whatever you are writing about each session, or leave the last sentence unfinished. This way you have a rolling start the following day.*

Q   I feel like I'm wasting time writing about random trivial things. When can I write my masterpiece?

A   *All in good time! These short sessions work wonders for your ability to write, keeping your creative juices flowing and your brain limbered up. On top of this, they train you to observe the all-important close detail that makes your work believable, and provide a mine of character sketches and detailed observations that you can return to in order to fine-tune your work.*

Q   It's so impersonal writing about everyday objects. It's not like I'm big-headed, but can't I just write about moi?

A   *You might be surprised just how much of what you have written about a random, impersonal object is related to your own unique experience of life. These short sessions will trigger off memories and thoughts long forgotten, allowing you to enrich your work.*

2

Taking the plunge

You may think your muse has passed you by, but it might be that she's the kind of girl who whispers rather than shouts. Ideas are everywhere, you just need to learn how to spot them.

So, you've cleared your desk, opened your notebook or a blank document on your computer, and are ready to write.

But suddenly your mind is devoid of inspiration and you begin to panic. What on earth are you going to write about? While there is more to being a writer than just a good idea, without an inspirational seed for your novel, screenplay or poem you are like a knight in armour with no monster to slay and no sweetheart to rescue.

BUSES

For many of us, ideas are a lot like buses. You wait ages for one to come along and when it finally does it breaks down. Then, when you're walking home in the rain, three more turn up and everybody else jumps on board. Of course you may be one of the lucky ones, and already be nurturing the seed of an idea. But for the majority of writers, it's a difficult truth that it takes more than motivation alone to produce a masterpiece.

Here's an idea for you...

Stuck for something to write about? Open your eyes and look around you. There is material everywhere. Read old diaries or browse through your notebooks. Read newspapers and magazines for fascinating stories. Sit in a café and gaze out of the window. Listen to conversations, invent stories for the people who walk past and write them down. It may take a while, but if you pay attention to the world around you, then inspiration will come. The trick is not to go looking for the idea of a lifetime. Sit back, relax, soak up your surroundings, listen to the scraps of thought that flutter through your brain and before you know it you'll be running round the block screaming 'Eureka!'.

DON'T IGNORE IT

If you have been inspired, don't ignore it. A great many writers turn away the ideas that flit around in the back of their head, begging to be put on paper. Why? Because the idea may not fit in with the self-image they want to nurture, or because they would like to write something more 'literary'. If you do this, you may be passing up a good thing. Don't ignore that persistent tug; take the bull by the horns and see where it leads.

The ideas that flutter in the half-light of our conscious mind are those that make us think, that make us laugh, or cry, or scream. Otherwise you would have forgotten them long ago. These ideas may be nothing more than a scene, a single character, perhaps something as small as a phrase. Or they might be an entire plot line, an epic journey that you have been mentally planning for years. But whether large or small, these threads are important to you, and because of this you have the ability to weave them into a work of art.

The writers I have known who have passed up these faint cries for attention have often gone on to pen strained and sterile work because the ideas they eventually work with don't engage them. Chances are, the ideas you may already possess, even if they are barely visible, have a personal significance. If you give them a chance, you will be able to draw on a wealth of personal emotion and experience in order to produce a literary work that truly connects with its readers.

The muse can often be encouraged to visit with a little playful experimentation. See IDEA 4, *Playing games*, for some suggestions.

Try another idea...

BUT...

But what happens if you are champing at the bit and raring to go, but have nothing to write about? Don't worry. Ideas are the product of your experience, bits of your life, inspiration from books, films, plays, all mingled together in a turbulent alchemical mix. This bubbling cauldron of images, words, sounds, smells and thoughts is constantly generating tendrils and strands that appear as random ideas or dreams. Occasionally these strike a chord in our mind and germinate to become inspiration. This isn't always a flash of pure genius, so learn to watch out for the little things, the tentative thoughts, the shy visions – chances are the smallest of seeds will grow into an idea if properly nurtured.

What this means is that although you may not have an idea per se, you do have a vast wealth of experience to draw upon. This bank of material is unique – the people you have loved, the places you have visited, the games you have played – nobody else has lived the same life. Start to peel back the years and look at the vast web of activity that is your life, and the ideas will begin to roll in.

'Experience is one thing you can get for nothing.'
OSCAR WILDE

Defining idea...

7

Q Fantastic! I've thought of an idea. But how do I know if it's any good?

A *There is no easy answer. Different readers like different things, and an almost infinite number of ideas have made it into good books. Perhaps the best way of determining the strength of your idea is to ask yourself (honestly) how you feel about it. It may be clever, but does it excite you? It may be exciting, but does it make sense? It may make sense, but is it original? At this stage, only you can answer these questions.*

Q Oh no! Every idea I come up with has been done before. There are no new ideas! Aaargh!

A *Calm down, breathe deeply and relax. We've all had moments like these. I have innocently penned several stories only to find out after I've submitted them that similar tales have already been published – often by famous writers who've written them much better than I have. How embarrassing. Of course the millions of books already in print use up an enormous number of ideas, but if you look closely, many bear close resemblance to one another. The truth is that even if your idea isn't original, your own unique way of writing and your own inimitable life experience will make the finished product one of a kind. If you like the idea, go for it.*

3

Second sight

We're all wearing blinkers, and like a plough-horse finally lifting its head to see the mountains, we've got to learn that there's more around us than mud. It's time to find our second sight.

Learn to see the world in a new light, a light that exposes sharp details and ironic truths. The view from your window just isn't enough — from now on, you'll be absorbing material everywhere you go.

SKETCHES

A book without detail is like a matchstick Mona Lisa. If what you are 'seeing' doesn't appear real, or lacks depth, then nobody will give it a chance. Detail is the skin of a literary work; it's what holds it together. It makes the background credible enough for it to become invisible (except, of course, when you want to draw attention to something), and allows your characters to stand out as fully rounded human beings. If you're too lazy to pad out your writing with telling details, then your project is in severe danger of becoming laughable rather than laudable.

Here's an idea for you...

Buy a notebook. Something small that can fit in your pocket or your handbag. When you see a detail that has some resonance with your work, jot it down. Don't stop with observations either, write down snatches of conversation, interesting news reports. Draw pictures of a car that one of your characters might own; items of clothing in shop windows that would make the perfect costume. The notebook will become a record of your own experience, and a scrapbook of what you consider to be important. The personal interest invested in these scraps will bring your work to life.

OBJECTION!

Most of us would claim to be observant people, but are we? Could we accurately describe the house across the street? The woman who works in the local wine shop? The route we follow to visit a loved one? We take a great deal of the world for granted because our brains automatically ignore anything that isn't immediately relevant, and as a result we become blind to the all-important details. I was shocked the other day when I couldn't remember the colour of my kitchen floor, despite it having remained unchanged for over ten years. I look at the floor every day, but I don't truly see it because it isn't an essential part of my life (which, I guess, I should be thankful for).

PEELING YOUR EYEBALLS

Disgusting image aside, this is exactly what you need to do in order to convert a featherweight piece of writing into a heavyweight champ. Don't take the world for granted. Look at things you wouldn't normally look at and see them in a new light. Notice the candle burning through the dirty window across the street, the scuffed and long-forgotten wedding ring embedded in the chubby, red finger of the woman in the wine shop, the angry graffiti that says 'love sucks' that you pass on the way to your loved one. It may be a cliché, but there is a story behind everything. Your job as a writer is to look for the detail that brings that story to light. Learning to see the little things will give your work a profound depth, and provide a constant torrent of fresh ideas, fascinating locations and vibrant characters.

Everyday objects don't have to stay ordinary for long – see IDEAS 5 and 12 for ways to vest even the most mundane of things with metaphorical meaning.

Try another idea...

Unless you are Marvin the Memory Man, don't rely on your noggin to store the newly uncovered details of your world. You may think you will remember a fascinating sight or unusual person later in the day, but chances are it will slip away and disappear forever. Most details are so small that they won't reside in your memory for more than a couple of minutes, although they could be part of the minutiae that make your book memorable for a lifetime. So always make notes, everywhere you go; be the annoying sod who's so busy scribbling that you bump into people on the street.

MAN OVERBOARD!

Of course, there is a limit to how much detail you can take in, and how much readers can put up with. It is good to be a detective, but don't become too forensic – think astute, not anal; *Kojak*, not *CSI*. To return to the same examples, the average reader isn't going to care how many bricks make up your neighbour's wall, or how many times the lady in the wine shop has to scan your scotch before it registers, or the type of asphalt on your loved one's drive (unless, of course, these things are actually relevant to the story). Note the details that say the most about your characters and their world, the particulars that reveal discrete but essential facts.

'Little minds are interested in the extraordinary; great minds in the commonplace.'
ELBERT HUBBARD, author and publisher

Defining idea...

13

How did
it go?

Q **I'm searching for the details in ordinary objects, but they just don't seem very exciting. Am I going wrong somewhere, or do I just need glasses?**

A *You need to search for the intimate details, rather than giving a mere physical description. Try and defamiliarise yourself from the actual object by noting down any memories or thoughts it inspires in you, or any feelings it may awaken in one of your characters.*

Q **I can't seem to find much to say about the world around me – it's like getting blood from a stone. How much detail can you extract from one small thing?**

A *A great deal! Pick a random object from your house, something you don't use much, then spend fifteen minutes writing about it. Look at it from every angle, note the way it looks, feels, tastes. Then write about it figuratively, what it reminds you of, whether it would make a good metaphor. Buy a good dictionary – building up your vocabulary will give you more control over the amount, and quality, of the detail in your work.*

Q **I've never really noticed the detail in the books I've read. Are you sure I need to worry about studying the minutiae?**

A *Next time you read a piece of creative poetry or prose take your time and work out how many sentences are there to provide detail, and which words help give you a strong sensory indication of the place or people. You'll be surprised at how much of a text is designed to paint a picture, and how that picture is designed to remain inconspicuous.*

4

Playing games

Down at the English faculty, creative writing is a serious business for serious people.

But writers don't want to work all of the time. Some simple game play can be fun and inspirational.

GET YOUR NOTEBOOKS OUT, IT'S TIME FOR A FEW GAMES...

I know you're here to write, and for many of you that will be a serious venture not to be undertaken lightly. Good, I'm glad you're committed; but no matter what you want to write about, or how spontaneous you want to be, it's always a good idea to practise some training exercises first. Even Miles Davis started off with scales before finding jazz.

FAR FROM AMUSING

How often have you stared at the ceiling appealing to your muse to pop down and bless you with inspiration? When I first started writing I was doing it all the time, spending afternoons alternately begging her to show up and cursing her for never doing so. I eventually realised that the poetic muse is shy. She likes to remain in the wings, out of the limelight. She'll wait until you're engrossed in other things, until

Here's an idea for you...

Try playing detective. Spend a day giving in to your most curious urges, your most nosy habits. Pretend that everywhere you go is your crime scene, that everyone around you is a suspect (although try not to follow people around, it could get you arrested). Look for the unusual in the everyday, the surprises in familiar landscapes, the unusual snippets of conversation from the people around you. When you find something fascinating, probe it, question it, interrogate it and imagine it. From this seemingly random bundle of information can be pulled the threads that form a poem or story.

your attention is elsewhere, then slip an idea into your head and disappear before you even know what's hit you.

Like her dental cousin, the poetic muse will sometimes appear when you're asleep: don't ignore those ideas that cling on after dreams – some excellent poems and stories have had their grounding in the weird world of sleep. If you want to encourage her to turn up more often, however, try playing games. And remember, inspiration isn't always an explosion. It can be a phrase, an image, even a word looked at from a new angle.

AN EXQUISITE CORPSE

Yes, it sounds creepy and disgusting (it was designed by the surrealists), but this oddly named game is one of the best tricks for developing your powers of expression and picking up strange new ideas. Get together with a few friends, not necessarily all writers. Now write a single line of poetry down at the top of a sheet of paper, fold it over so it can't be seen, and hand it to the next person who does the same thing. If you get a lot of people taking part you can end up with some fascinatingly surreal poems, but as long as there are at least two of you the results will be worthwhile and hilarious.

One variation on this is for the first player to write down an article and an adjective (the skinny) and fold the paper, the second person then writes a noun (marmoset), the third person writes a transitive verb (runs up), the fourth another article and adjective (the bleeding), and the fifth one last noun (sock). You end up with some rib-tickling sentences. They may not make much sense, but by playing around with random ideas you often find yourself tapping into your unconscious and finding inspiration.

Looking doesn't always mean seeing – look at IDEA 3, *Second sight*, for ways to peel your eyeballs.

Try another idea...

ENGLISH LESSONS

Obviously there won't be many of you who don't speak English, unless you just bought this book for the pretty cover. But no matter how well you think you know your mother tongue, don't take it for granted. Those twenty-six letters may seem innocuous but they have the power to create anything you want, anything you can imagine, and your job as a writer is to make the alphabet speak in an original and surprising way.

Think of a child's abecedary (A is for Apple, B is for Bee,...). Now try writing one for grown-ups, thinking of unusual words for each letter, concrete or abstract nouns, verbs or adjectives. Focus on creating a particular tone: light-hearted, sinister, condescending – it's up to you. After each entry, write another short phrase based on whatever the image conjures, so you end up with something along the lines of 'A is for absolution; asked for but never given'. Another interesting game to play, based on a poem by John Updike, is to use 26 adjectives, each beginning with a different letter, to characterise 26 people. Use as many different words as you like, but the central description has to be based around that adjective.

'Anything is fit material for poetry.'
WILLIAM CARLOS WILLIAMS

Defining idea...

17

How did it go?

Q   I know poems are short, but should I really be reeling them off in five minutes? How long should it take me to write a poem?

A   Just because some poems are short doesn't mean they take minutes to write. The time it takes to write a poem varies from person to person, and poem to poem. Never try and rush your writing – focus on the content, not the clock.

Q   I'm not really much of a game player – my Dad always told me to work not play and we lived in a strict 'no ball games' area. Can't I just start writing?

A   When playing these games, you'll feel less pressure than you do when simply sitting down to write. Because of this, your expectations of what you can achieve are lower. This enables you to relax, and open up your mind to new ideas. Just allow yourself the freedom to play with ideas. You're also more likely to write well once you've warmed up a little first.

Q   I've been following people around all day, and I've had loads of weird looks but no ideas. What am I doing wrong?

A   Are you looking closely enough at the people around you? Even if all you get are weird looks, use that as inspiration. Write a sketch about why a character would get weird looks, what they are doing to deserve them, what's odd about them. Edgar Allan Poe wrote a story about a man in a crowd; try it yourself. Even if you don't get any solid ideas, the practice of observing and collecting detail will really help you define your work once you start writing.

5

Shall I compare thee to a summer's day?

How do you stop the big things from having little meaning and the little things from getting too big and messy? Confused? Me too.

There was a time when literary convention dictated that only certain subjects were fit for poetry. You could write about love, death and beauty, but if you wanted to tackle any other issues you pretty much had to ditch the verse and write a report.

Today, thankfully, things have changed. I've reviewed poems on every conceivable subject, from woodlice to iPods, medieval warfare to cypress trees, and while not every piece worked (or even made sense, for that matter), it proves there's no excuse for a lack of topics to write about.

Here's an idea for you...

Make two lists: the first containing locations (a bathroom, a garage, a church) and the second containing abstract terms (love, anger, madness). Randomly pick a word from each list to make an abstract location, say 'the bathroom of madness'. Now write a short poem or prose piece describing the place, without using any abstract words (even the one you picked). The idea is to convey the feel of a place using the evidence of your senses and the truth of your own experience and not have to rely on meaningless, shadowy abstraction.

FIRE!

How do you know if an idea is suitable for a poem? Any idea, however faint, that gets you excited, that touches a nerve, or evokes an emotional response can be the spark of inspiration. The trick now is to fan that spark with enough strength to create a fire without flapping so much you blow it out. The biggest pitfall is going for the big topics such as love, death, time, nature and god without sufficient preparation. All poets tackle some of these subjects at some point – it's why poetry exists, and it would be unusual if you didn't want to at least try and explain through verse the issues that mystify you. But in order to capture the essence of these abstract phrases you need to know how to keep it personal.

GET A GRIP

When you embark on a poem that deals with love, or any other abstract term, you're always in danger of obscurity and repetition. The word love isn't tied to anything specific, it's different for each and every person, and nobody can pin down exactly what it feels like. Moreover, when writing (or reading) about love you suddenly find yourself bombarded with each and every love poem you've ever heard, which further loosens your grasp on the term. So when you use the word love in your poetry the image it tends to create is a shadowy, muffled one. The more abstract and high-flown the phrase, the less precise and evocative it will be. Try to avoid abstract terms altogether in your writing – it's difficult to empathise with a vague impression.

Symbolism can vest the most ordinary of things with an incredible depth of meaning. IDEA 12, *That's so abstract, dude*, gives some more ideas about making the abstract personal.

Try another idea...

KEEP IT PERSONAL

So how can you convey an abstraction without referring to it directly? With subtle, personal hints rather than a slap in the face. Instead of using a poem to tell a reader about a terrifying experience, show them. In other words, don't use the word terrified (a reader's eyes will brush over it, it means nothing to them in the context of your poem), but try and convey the experience of being terrified – how you felt, what you were thinking. Everybody has been terrified at some point in their life, and if you evoke the way you were affected by the experience you can attract a reader's empathy.

THE OBJECTIVE CORRELATIVE

Say what now? Yes, it's a tricky phrase to get your lips round, but then it was one of T. S. Eliot's. What he was referring to was the need

'Storytelling reveals meaning without committing the error of defining it.'
HANNAH ARENDT, political philosopher

Defining idea...

to transfer an abstract emotion onto a real, solid object. It's no use just bandying words like love and death around. You need to tie them down to a concrete 'thing' so that they acquire a physical presence: they become real emotions experienced by real people.

I'm not necessarily talking about metaphors here: to write a poem about an old man visiting a cemetery might involve a headstone as a metaphor for the

21

inevitability of death. This is a fairly obvious symbolic link. Instead, the same old man may be looking through his dead wife's wardrobe for things he can donate to charity and come across a tatty pair of shoes she wore forty years ago. The shoes aren't a direct metaphor, but they embody the sadness he feels at her passing. Through the object you can evoke a powerful, terrifying feeling of loss; the painful flood of returning memories; the distant abstract made flesh and soul. This is how powerful writing is born.

How did it go?

Q   Bugger. So I'm not allowed to use abstract terms to convey emotion. But I can still use good old sentimentality, right?

A   *There's no denying that a poem is a method of conveying your feelings. But don't resort to doing so with sentimentality. When you hear Westlife on the radio singing about how you're the only one they'll ever love do you believe them? Sentimental verse like this doesn't seem real (unless you're thirteen years old) because we are aware it's designed to manipulate us. In order for any kind of verse to attract empathy it has to convince the reader that it is sincere. Just as with abstract terms, stop yourself from sentimentalising your poem's emotional content – try and uncover what you're feeling, and what associations it conjures. Avoid grandeur and insincerity at all times – if you're not emotionally engaged with your writing, no reader will be. Rely on the details to convey mood and tone, don't simply tell people what to feel.*

Q   Oh, then what about generalisation?

A   *Do you even have to ask?*

6

Blowing your trumpet

If you're like me, some days you probably think there isn't much floating around in the memory department of your brain except for a few old episodes of *Thundercats*. But learn to dive in deeper – your past can be the key to great writing.

I'll bet when Proust was dipping his pastries in his tea that morning the last thing he expected was his whole life to flash before his eyes.

Yet this goes to show just how many memories there are in each of us, a vast tidal wave of experience that could break at any time and flood back into our present consciousness. These memories – these stories – are what give us the power to write realistically and evocatively. The key is learning how to harness them.

YESTERDAY...

All your troubles seemed so far away. And not just your troubles either. Memory is like that: how are you supposed to recapture events or conversations that now exist only in the murky depths of your mind? I don't know about you, but my memory is hopeless. I find it hard to remember what I was doing last week, let alone last year (and unfortunately this has nothing to do with alcohol). But my memory, or more

Here's an idea for you... **Your memory may well need a kick-start. Start by picking some random moments from your past, something like your first day at school, or your first kiss. When you have chosen five or six, write what you remember about the experience. Don't search for particular memories or precise detail, just write whatever comes to mind (and remember, avoid abstract terms). Do this for twenty minutes then read back what you've written.**

precisely my history, is the foundation of who I am. When Wordsworth said that the child was the father of the man, he was emphasising that the sum of your past experience, including your childhood, is what makes you uniquely you.

KEEPING TRACK

I compensate for my fuzzy mind by keeping diaries. They're nothing special. Most entries are random observations from events or meetings rather than detailed accounts of treasured moments. These scraps of text only mention the odd scent, like Charlie Red on a date, or a tune, like 'Abide With Me' from a funeral. But I don't need any more than that to remember the event. The senses are the key to unlocking your memories. How many times has a taste or smell dragged you back to a precise moment in your past, often so unexpectedly that you have to gasp for breath? Powerful fiction is based on thoughtful use of all of the senses and the emotional memories they evoke.

MEMORY TRANSPLANTS

These sudden, immensely powerful flashbacks are an essential part of writing, and can be miracle cures for a text that is lacking in emotional or descriptive depth. Of course a piece of writing that only features your memories is autobiography, and won't always interest a reader, but they will enable you to paint a much more vivid picture of your characters and their setting.

Your memories enable to you to construct an image that is unique to you, that resonates with your own history, even if ostensibly the plot you're working on seems a million miles away. This attention to detail, this engagement with elements from your past, can be transplanted from your mind to that of your characters, creating a much stronger illusion of real people. Incorporating the memorable sights, smells, tastes, sounds and touches that mean so much to you will create a tangible atmosphere in your work, one that might feel like a real memory to everybody that reads it, as well as to you. Building memories into writing is a key to writing powerfully, it is why something that isn't real can have the strength of something that is.

For more hints on how to use your world – your home, your history, your surroundings – in your work, see IDEA 31, *There's no place like home.*

Try another idea...

LOOKING BACK

It's always fascinating to look at what the mind remembers when asked to do so spontaneously. What about your five senses: which seems most important? Visual, most likely, but what other sensory reminders come into play? And how do you express your emotional experience of an event? Look for the strings of associations in your mind that help memories flood back to the present. When they do, make notes, capture the salient details, and allow your mind to follow along the path the memories lead: where were you, what were you doing, how were you feeling? Expand and write a little about yourself and the people you knew back then. What's changed? These 'oh yeah, I'd forgotten about that!' moments are the details that can be inserted into your work to make it that much more convincing.

'Anybody who has survived an average childhood has enough to write about for a dozen years.'
FLANNERY O'CONNOR, US writer

Defining idea...

27

How did it go?

Q **Oh God, I hate being put under pressure! What events should I be trying to remember? I can't think of any!**

A *Stop being lazy – pick anything! But if you're really stuck, try one of the following. Your first memory; your first day at school; your first kiss; your first journey; your first bedroom; your first pet; your first experience of death; a memorable item of clothing or shoes; the most evocative smell/taste/sound you can remember; the most memorable person you no longer see.*

Q **I'm thinking back to my past, it's getting clearer. I think I can see something...yes, it's...aaaargh! I'd managed to repress that thought and now it's back – you bastard!**

A *Sorry, don't hate me! You may find the same memories or the same themes recurring in your work. Don't ignore them, even if they are memories you want to leave hidden. These pieces of your past are providing the fuel for powerful writing. Harness them, listen to them, and you may even begin to see it as a form of therapy.*

Q **My memory is pretty awful, and I can't quite remember which bits are real and which bits I've made up. Does this blurring of fact, fiction and history really matter?**

A *We all contribute to and elaborate our history as we get older, in many cases remembering something completely differently from the way it actually happened (according to my partner, this happens to me all the time). It doesn't matter if what you remember isn't entirely real: you're writing creative fiction! As long as it feels real to you, then it will make evocative reading. Emotional truth is what's important.*

7

Digging the dirt

Research. It's for academics and non-fiction writers, right? Wrong. Your imagination is what drives a piece of writing, but you really need to do your homework if you want to look convincing.

My primary school English teacher used to tell us all to 'write about what we know', especially when we were feeling adventurous and attempting to describe something new.

This really bugged me, and the sad truth is that if everybody had a teacher like that then the literary world would have little to offer. When you're a kid writing about space wars and Indiana Jones-style adventure you are writing about what you know because you are emotionally engaged with your subject. And this doesn't change just because you've grown up: it's your world, so keep dreaming.

STAY SHARP

OK, so some things do change when you grow up. When you are young, your stories are rarely grounded in everyday physics. Space stations don't run out of oxygen, and your intrepid hero is usually impervious to every weapon under the sun. When you

Here's an idea for you... **If you are writing about a character with an unfamiliar vocation then set yourself a week to try to learn everything about their craft and their workplace. Visit libraries and bookshops, or read other novels with the same subject. The internet is a vast store of easily accessible research material, so get surfing. Write short paragraphs describing a character's day at work, how he feels, what she does. Try using different levels of technical language until you find the right balance. After a few days you'll find that not only do you know your character more intimately, but your powers of description should have improved too.**

are writing as an adult, and when you truly want people to take your work seriously, you have to start obeying nature's rules. Your readers aren't always going to want to suspend their disbelief indefinitely (although there are exceptions), so physics reasserts itself.

LET'S GET PHYSICAL

A later professor of mine, who was also a writer, told me that my teacher's comment was right, but in the wrong way. To 'write what you know', he said, 'means do your research'. A little background reading can make even the most obscure science fiction story appear plausible, allowing a reader to focus on the characters and the plot rather than raise an eyebrow at the logistics. And it isn't just science fiction authors that need research. Practically every piece of writing, whether poetry, prose or drama, will benefit from being well informed, and it could make the difference between a finished piece that lacks credibility and depth and one that effectively transports your reader to a new place or time.

THE GOOD NEWS...

For those of you who are concerned that research is arduous, tedious and the antithesis of everything spontaneous writing should be, take comfort in the fact that it doesn't always involve libraries and dusty tomes. Essentially there are two forms of research – internal and external. The former is the kind most writers like best, because you can do it practically anywhere you like. In fact, the more common term for internal research is daydreaming. It is vital, when writing anything, to be able to fully imagine your characters – the way they behave, interact with others, respond to the world around them and their changing circumstances.

Creating a believable setting in your work is vital: check out IDEAS 28, *Virtual reality* and 29, *Changing rooms* for some tips.

Try another idea...

In order to do this, close your eyes and imagine your characters in as many different situations as possible. Try to picture what the world looks like through their eyes, how they would act in a variety of situations. Work out biographies for them, events from their past, people they have loved and lost. Do this at work, on the bus, in the bath, on the toilet, and remember – write it down! Much of the craft of writing is spent in this manner, quietly building up a mental image of your characters and their world. It may not seem like you're working, but the truth is that if you can't picture your characters, nobody else will.

...AND THE BAD

It is sad but true that even if your characters are deeper than the Mariana Trench they will appear pancake-like if their world lets them down. Your fictional settings need to be realistic. And while sometimes this can be achieved by staying alert to the world around you, the chances are that part of what you are writing about will be unfamiliar territory. You may be dying to start writing, but take the time to learn more about the world you are trying to describe and the people you want in it. It may take a while, and you may not even use it all, but it is a vital part of painting a realistic landscape.

'To imagine yourself inside another person...is what a story writer does in every piece of work; it is his first step, and his last too, I suppose.'
EUDORA WELTY, US writer

Defining idea...

How did it go?

Q **Well, I've been accused of being a stalker but I finally know everything there is to know about my character's profession. But why does my writing now seem a little stale?**

A *You don't want to end up just writing a handbook for your character's job. When researching, you should be aiming to build up a picture of your character in your mind. Most of the information you collect won't be used in your work, instead it will help give a clearer image of your creations, their mindset, how they feel about the world and how they choose to live. Researching the everyday points of somebody's life is a way to unlock the kind of person they are, and how they feel about the bigger picture, as well as making them come alive on the page.*

Q **I'm a bit of a sci-fi junkie and I'm writing about a world with some damn strange mechanical nick-nacks. Do I still have to research the technical details, or can I just make them up?**

A *Do you really need to ask? OK, with some fantasy or sci-fi books you can get away with making up the scientific stuff, but it still has to be at least based on something that's real, either physically or theoretically. Even the Enterprise's warp drive was based on a plausible form of space propulsion. The fact is that putting in a bit of research, even if it's just a phrase or two here or there, can give you a great deal of authority as a writer. Read Dan Brown's* The Da Vinci Code *to see how effective research can be.*

8

When the rhythm starts to play

Life is full of natural rhythms – just try walking to an irregular beat and you'll be falling over yourself in no time. You don't have to write sonnets to get rhythm into your poetry, just keep your ears open to nature's pulse.

If you're like the vast majority of poets out there, you probably started writing without thinking too hard about metre.

You may have vague recollections of 'iambic pentameter' from school but you may not quite recall what counting syllables has to do with self-expression. You certainly don't need to write trochees or spondees in order to craft good poetry, but finding your own rhythm is a vital step to making your work your own, and stopping it resembling your dad on the dance floor.

A SECTION THAT DESCRIBES PENTAMETER

Knowing how to use rhythm in poetry doesn't require a degree. In fact, all you have to do is look at everyday speech. Take the heading above, for instance: 'a section that describes pentameter'. It's made up of ten alternating strong and weak

Take a piece of spoken or written text and break it down into a poem. Sounds odd, but give it a chance: it'll help you get to grips with the way a poem's rhythm determines its shape. Read the text and work out its rhythm. Speak it aloud. Now write it out as a poem, without changing the words themselves. Use your instinct to determine where the line breaks should be, and look closely at how your choices affect the character, tone and meaning of the text. It may take a while to get right, but eventually you should be able to turn prose into a convincing piece of poetry.

syllables. This is actually an iambic pentameter: one of the most commonly used metrical systems in poetry, adopted by such luminaries as Milton and Wordsworth. You don't have to speak like Shakespeare in order to write in iambic pentameter – your language can be modern and natural and still be set to that pace – but the rhythm helps order the words, working to make them more fluent, and give them more impact, than those without structure.

RHYTHM HELPS YOUR TWO HIPS MOVE

Some academics make metre sound like a science, but nobody actually reads poetry in this fractured, halting way. In fact, it's best, for now, to forget about metre (as something a poet imposes on their words) and start thinking about rhythm – the musical movement and flow of speech.

If the word rhythm makes you think of steel drums and samba, great! It's all about movement, music, freedom; what Robert Frost calls the 'abstract vitality of our speech'. Try to listen to the way people talk without actually hearing what they're saying. Don't focus on the words, tune in to the stresses, the intonation (the rise and fall of pitch) and the voice quality.

Make that your task for this week: go out and listen to the music and rhythm of language. Listen to people on the bus, in the pub, on television, listen to yourself. But hear the noise, not the words – tune the meaning out (a great technique to learn for next time you have an argument with a loved one). We're lucky in that English is a language in which strong and weak stresses alternate in a fairly evenly distributed way. Next time you're writing, try and convey these patterns onto the page as honestly as possible: you'll probably find a rhythm emerging. The most important thing is to always go with your instincts: if your heart breaks rhythm you see a doctor, if your footsteps fall out of sync you fall over, if a line doesn't feel like it's got a natural rhythm, you change it.

Another way of sensing a poem's rhythm is by reading it out aloud – IDEA 10, *Style is everything*, will give you some tips.

Try another idea...

FEEL FREE

In short, it doesn't matter if you go traditional and strike up an iambic pose, or break out and listen to the natural rhythms of everyday speech – you have to have an underlying beat of some sort. Even free verse, with no discernible metre, has rhythm. Writing poetry without rhythm, says Frost, is like 'playing tennis with the net down'. Experiment with different kinds of metre, but don't just rebel against it because you feel it might be restrictive: remember, one of the primary principles of poetry is organisation. Keep playing until you find your own balance between the underlying order of metre and the natural rhythm of spoken language. Once you've found this rhythm, your lines will always have energy and life.

'Find me good poems without rhythm. Find me warm-blooded life without breathing.'
GEOFFREY GRIGSON, poet and critic

Defining idea...

35

How did it go?

Q   **I hear what you're saying about rhythm, but is there any way of using this advice for a poem that's already been written? Some of my old work is so devoid of rhythm that even my dad's embarrassed to read it out loud!**

A   *Of course. One of my favourite techniques is to take a poem I'm not happy with and slice it up into phrases or lines. Use a large piece of paper as your table and go mad: rearrange the parts of your poem until you no longer recognise it. Then work with these snippets, try them out in different patterns, different shapes, all the time trying to pin down a rhythm that feels right. It may end up a complete mess (so remember to keep an original), but this experimentation can give you a fresh outlook on a poem and help you create a satisfying rhythm.*

Q   **OK, I'm trying your prose-to-poetry exercise but I'm coming across the same problem I always face when writing poetry – how do I know where to put my line breaks?**

A   *There are no rules other than to listen to that inner voice: does the layout contribute to the rhythm or break it up; does it make the poem easier, or harder, to read? The first and last words of a line influence a poem's rhythm, pacing, momentum and above all meaning, so think carefully about what you're trying to convey.*

9

There once was a man from Kentuckett...

When I started writing poetry, I never knew how to shape it on the page. I could never decide where to break the bloody lines and so it always ended up as prose. Thankfully, finding the right form for self-expression is easier than you think.

With poetry, finding your voice and getting it down on paper can seem an impossible task.

You may be working with the medium in order to express yourself, to explore hidden facets of your personality. All well and good. But if you can't learn to shape this torrential subject matter it'll probably end up as nonsense, not verse. I bet you want to leap right in and write something that outshines *The Waste Land*, but take your time, breathe deeply and learn to play a little before you start to get serious.

USING YOUR HEAD

Chances are that when you start writing poetry you stick to your own rhythm. Expressing yourself can be hard enough without having to do so to the beat of somebody else's drum. There's nothing wrong with this: if you know the rhythm of

Here's an idea for you... **If you're having trouble getting a structured poem down on paper, try writing it as a sonnet or even a haiku. Once you stop worrying about *how* you're saying things, you'll be able to focus on *what* you're saying. Once you've pinned it down, you can try again with your own structure.**

your voice, then you can write powerful poetry with a structure all of your own.

But there's a fine line between a poem and a ramble, and if you don't pay attention to your poem's structure, it's in danger of becoming like one of my mum's cakes: so loose it falls apart. It may appear easier to express yourself without the limitations of a traditional structure, but this attitude can be deceiving. Left to ponder shape, how can you pin down exactly what it is you're feeling, precisely which elements of your turbulent inner voice to capture on paper? Writing to a traditional form may seem restrictive, but it can actually free your mind by creating a structure for you. When you don't have to worry about structure, you can devote more of your creative energy to playing with content.

MAKING INROADS

Too many people try to write a beautifully crafted epic poem on their first go. It's like waking up one morning and deciding you're going to win Olympic gold in judo, although the only tussle you've ever had is trying to wrestle open your Pop Tarts. As a poet, you need to become more aware of the fascinating and surprising powers of language to awaken long-lost ideas and memories, and the best way to do this is to start small.

Look at the fragments of ideas and phrases in your notebook and play with them. Don't try and craft a masterpiece just yet, simply start scribbling, write without thinking and see where it leads. Automatic writing, as it's often called, doesn't have to make sense – in fact, the more arbitrary your subject the better the results. The idea is to open up your unconscious mind, which is such an important part of writing poetry, and to practise using this vast resource of feeling and emotion. By starting small, by tuning your mental antennae for unexpected resonances, moods and memories, poems will begin to shape themselves in no time.

Rhyme is one means of keeping a poem clean. See IDEA 40, *Yakety yak*, to stop your structure getting naughty.

Try another idea...

MODEL LOOKS

If you're having trouble finding inspiration for your poems, or can't seem to knock them into shape, the answer may lie in imitation. Think of it as a kind of flattery. Philip Larkin, for example, claimed that when he started out he always had a copy of Yeats on his kitchen table next to his open notebook. Try imitating a poet you've always admired. Don't blatantly transplant lines from famous poems into your work, but do take a close look at a poem that really moves you and try working out why.

Next, try writing one of your own that has a similar structure, rhythm or theme. Using models is an excellent way to practise probing into the depths of your creativity and to gain a comprehensive feel for language and form. Just remember that imitation alone won't make you a great poet. Think of it as riding on the shoulders of a mentor: they can only carry you so far, then you have to make your own way. If you carry on using other poems as models, you'll never be able to get your own unique voice on the page.

'A poem is never a thought to begin with. It is at its best when it is a tantalising vagueness. It finds its thought and succeeds or it doesn't find it and comes to nothing.'
ROBERT FROST

Defining idea...

How did
it go?

Q   **I love the idea of employing a model (poem, that is), but I'm a little nervous about using a master like Yeats. Does it have to be someone so...challenging?**

A   *Good lord no! Yeats is a fantastic poet but it's often best to start with somebody a little more contemporary and a tad more approachable. Pick somebody whose poems you empathise with, someone whose work moves you. Try looking at poets such as Carol Ann Duffy, Ramona Herdman or Elizabeth Bishop.*

Q   **I'm going to try and get to grips with a model (yes, I'm still talking about poetry), but using a whole poem is a little daunting. Can I start off with something smaller?**

A   *If you don't feel comfortable using a whole poem, pick the first line from some of your favourites and continue writing. It might just be the inspiration you need to craft something unique. For a change, pick a last line and work backwards. If it's 'they'd fizz like dead TV, unreel like falling snow' (from a poem by Ramona Herdman) ask yourself what associations the image conjures, what emotions. Probe the line until an idea grabs you, then follow it and write a poem of your own, paying attention to the way the content forms itself on the page. When doing this, it's usually best if you haven't read the rest of the poem – you want the ideas to be your own.*

10

Style is everything!

The style you choose to write in can say an awful lot about you. Don't be shy and don't be false, just act natural: like your sense of dress, your writing style should be personal and unique to you.

'Style is everything.' I'm sure most of you have heard that before. I heard it all the time at school from the lads decked in cool Reebok trainers (tongue pulled out) and fashionable fluorescent shell suits.

No matter how much you try and convince yourself, style in any walk of life is important, and whether poetry or prose, readers respond to style as much as subject matter. But in order to write persuasively, that style has to reflect your true self.

WORD UP

You can't ignore the fact that literary texts are made up of words, and the choice of which words to use and why – style – is one of the fundamental questions posed by any writer. With the ability to say the same thing countless different ways, what do

Here's an idea for you... **Read your work aloud. You don't have to read it to anybody, just do what Yeats did and pace back and forth reading to yourself. Listen for any discomfort in the language, any words that don't sound right, any clichés you didn't spot when writing. And listen to the shape of it, how well it rolls off the tongue, how well each line works and whether they combine to make a well-rounded whole. You may feel a little silly talking to yourself, but it's worth it.**

we hope to achieve by picking one over the other? It's like deciding what to wear when you step outside – you want your clothes to say something about you to whoever you're meeting. When writing, you want the style to reflect what you're trying to say. You wouldn't try and put a serious message across in a limerick, just as you wouldn't turn up for a meeting with your publisher wearing just your underwear.

DRESS NATURAL

Your writing style – like your dress sense – will probably have a great deal to do with your personality. You might embark on a piece of writing using the language of your neighbourhood, or your childhood, a style of speaking that's extremely familiar to you and highly colloquial on the page. You might be aiming for something more sophisticated, mixing a higher register of speech in with your familiar vocal patterns. Or you may be trying a completely different style, one as far removed from everyday speech as possible using language you've picked up from books or research.

It's up to you what style you want to use, but try to stay true to yourself. I know that sounds a little new age, but if you try to write in a style that you're not comfortable with, simply because you want to create a more literary effect, you risk sounding false. That doesn't mean don't play around with new registers – try every style imaginable: humble, simple, rude, posh, learned, scientific, nonsense, arcane – but if you start including words that really don't fit in with your style, or feel you're straining to keep up a certain tone of language, it's best to pause and evaluate what message or mood you're trying to convey.

Style is who you are, it reflects the kind of person you've chosen to be. See IDEA 6, *Blowing your trumpet*, for ways of exploring your past and getting to know yourself.

Try another idea...

KEEP IT REAL

Quite a few writers try and elevate the style of their writing unnecessarily, often to try and impress a lover/professor/parent. But more often than not the result comes across as artificial: this isn't the writer speaking honestly, it's literary window-dressing. Drop the act, and just be yourself.

The trick to succeeding is quite simply to stop trying so hard. Don't try and be different, don't try and be clever. If you're reaching for your thesaurus every five minutes and trying to fit in words like antidisestablishmentarianism your sentences or lines will end up like sticky cement, and a reader won't enjoy traipsing through them. Remember, writing is about communication – use language that you're comfortable with, and your readers will feel comfortable too. Powerful writing uses the living, breathing language of everyday speech. And for the more experimental poets among you, writing with everyday language doesn't mean creating everyday poetry: just look at e. e. cummings.

'Style is life! It is the very life blood of thought!'
GUSTAVE FLAUBERT

Defining idea...

How did it go?

Q **Whenever Beckham changes his hair I follow suit. Is it OK for me to emulate other people's writing style in the same way?**

A *If you read a great deal when writing it's often tempting to try to reproduce the elements of a text that you enjoy. This respectful admiration is fine, and trying to emulate another writer when you first start out can be a useful way to experiment with other styles. Try as many different styles as you like, your own unique way of writing will probably evolve from these exercises. However, emulation can be restrictive if you come to rely on it. You want your work to be your own, not lost in someone else's shadow.*

Q **I'm always being told I'm a bossy boots. It's OK to adopt a didactic style in your poetry, isn't it?**

A *The same points can also be applied to lecturing when writing: don't try too hard to convince people of what you're trying to say. If you make your message too explicit, people will feel they're being dictated to. Trust yourself to pick out the right details to convey your message more subtly and with greater power.*

Q **Can I flirt with those bad boys postmodernism and experimentation?**

A *It's OK to play around with new ways of writing, but don't rupture and fragment your text with flashy tricks just to look as though you've discovered something new. This structural play isn't originality, it's only a way of avoiding the need to create realistic characters and develop your own style. Natural writing isn't synonymous with boring writing, but experimental writing often is. Have faith in your own unique way of writing. Your own voice may take time to come, but it will.*

11

A sensuous, transcendent, sublime chapter

Language is a powerful device. You can use it to create any thing or mood you want. Ensuring that every word is efficiently placed and full of meaning is the first step towards writing that really packs a punch.

The English language is like the best pick 'n' mix you can imagine. We've got an unrivalled collection of words — the legacy of a couple of millennia of conquest and capitulation.

But this variety has its cons as well as its pros. Just like a chef who has too many ingredients in his kitchen and makes up a chocolate and duck breast soufflé with tarragon and peanut butter syrup sauce served with fried Mars Bars and offal, a writer who makes too much of the language's finer points risks cooking up a dish that nobody can stomach.

SIMPLER IS BETTER

Sticking to the gastronomic metaphors, one of my pet hates is fancy food. I've been to a few restaurants in my time, and what I can't stand is when the chef dishes up a sliver of

Here's an idea for you... **Take a piece of your work and strike through every adjective and adverb with a pencil. Then, look through carefully and remove the lines from those words that actually contribute to the text, rather than confuse it. Alternatively, write a short story or scene using no adverbs or qualifiers and only one well-placed adjective and see what the effect is.**

ridiculously decorated food, trussed up in expensive salad leaves and drizzled with geometrically perfect lines of balsamic vinegar. And then charges a small fortune for it. It may taste nice, but it's gone before it even hits the sides, and leaves you feeling hungry for something more substantial (usually a kebab on the way home).

Words work in the same way. If you go for something too fancy you risk losing any sense of meaning or substance, and leaving a reader craving something with a little more meat. Part of the problem can be the huge range and variety of words to choose from, but when writing try and remember to go for the hearty stew, not the parma ham salad: in other words, choose Saxon words over Romance ones. Saxon words are those that turn up most frequently in everyday language, the ones we choose to communicate to each other with. Romance words are those that stem from Latin, the ones that turn up in Renaissance sonnets, and which appear more 'posh'. Sticking to familiar words will make you more friends.

TONGUE TWISTERS

In the same vein, try not to let your sentences get out of control. Circumlocution, when you speak in circles, is one thing that will really get on a reader's nerves. Always try and get your point across concisely and precisely. If you start penning untidy, rambling sentences readers will wonder if you're making any point at all.

The same with tautology: there's no need to say things twice or even three times – 'the chicken crossed to the other side of the road' is just a clumsier version of 'the chicken crossed the road'.

Adjectives and adverbs are tricky sods alright, but not half as tricky as abstract phrases. IDEA 12, *That's so abstract, dude*, gives some words of caution.

Try another idea...

DON'T BE FOOLED

Adjectives are a fool's gold. They seem so easy, so apt, they look like they'll fit in to your work so well. Sometimes, yes, but too many adjectives and your work will end up losing meaning, not focusing it. If I opened a book with 'Adam was a tall, dark, well-dressed man' I'm not really saying anything. How tall is tall? What's dark, his skin or his hair? What qualifies as being well dressed? Adjectives don't always produce a precise image, a picture that a reader can work with; instead they just produce a list of vague descriptions. Make sure that you use adjectives sparsely, and only when they really say something.

The same applies to adverbs – any word which conditions a verb, pinning down its quality. Don't be lazy and write 'he ran quickly to the car'; there is a vast store of verbs in the English language, each of which produces a different and precise image. Try 'he sprinted' or 'he dashed' or 'he jogged', it conjures a much more powerful sense of movement and motive. Scrap any adverbs that you don't need – like 'she tiptoed quietly'. There's no need for these, all they do is weaken your narrative and make editors wince.

'Substitute "damn" every time you're inclined to write "very"; your editor will delete it and the writing will be just as it should be.'
MARK TWAIN

Defining idea...

How did it go?

Q I know now that adjectives and adverbs are the devil's children, so should I just try and avoid them altogether?

A I would never recommend this level of restriction when writing normally – when used wisely, adjectives, adverbs and qualifiers can help tighten and focus a piece of writing, and a piece of work with none would feel strange. What I want you to do is learn which words benefit your work and which weaken it, and the above exercise is a great way to look at how thoughtless descriptive words can ruin a piece of writing. You want every word to combine like some fantastic, well-oiled machine; to pack a punch, not a paunch. Getting rid of all of this dead wood will enable the reader to surf across your words, not drown in them.

Q I've got rid of unwanted adjectives and adverbs, but there's still some dead wood clouding up my work. Is there anything else I can chuck at the waste bin?

A One last thing to avoid is the qualifier – any word that restricts or modifies the meaning of another word or phrase. These include 'fairly', 'often', 'quite' and so on. Unless they are absolutely essential (in other words, the meaning of a sentence changes considerably if they are removed) they will only lessen the impact and strength of your writing. E. B. White says it best: 'Rather, very, little, pretty – these are the leeches that infest the pond of prose, sucking the blood of words.'

12

That's so abstract, dude

Writing is about exploring the parts of yourself you don't really understand; grappling with what it means to be human. To do this, you need a more powerful arsenal to work with than a few abstract terms.

Life is immeasurably complex, and no human being can be expected to comprehend the subtleties of existence.

Yet the brain is a truly breathtaking miracle of engineering. Despite the fact that the experience of living seems beyond the mere descriptive powers of words, we can still use language to explain ourselves to ourselves, and to grasp the essence of what it is to be alive.

BAD WORDS

Of course there are words apparently designed to be able to embody the depths of experience and emotion; words that crop up again and again in narratives, that we hear every day. But these words – love, hate, confusion, fear, anger, insecurity, even feeling – are charlatans. On the surface they seem to embody a precise, powerful image, one that you can instantly recognise. But look a little deeper and they are hollow, and all too ready to disappear before you can get a grip on their meaning.

Here's an idea for you... **Write down an abstract emotion in the middle of a blank page, then around it write down the things you associate with it. Try looking at it from as many different perspectives as possible – try and describe it through all your senses. What are your strongest memories of the feeling? If the abstract emotion was an object/animal/person what would it be? Avoid clichés: keep your associations personal and they will keep their potency.**

No, it isn't these words that enable us to understand the world and our place in it.

GOOD WORDS

When we're trying to explain the intricacies of life to ourselves, or when we're writing (often the same thing), the use of generalised abstract phrases clouds our thoughts rather than clarifying them. Trying to describe the experience of fear by using the word fear accomplishes nothing, because the word fear is so general as to be meaningless. It all sounds a little confusing, I know, but the essence of what I'm trying to say is that our aim when writing is to make abstract concepts appear concrete and realistic on the page, and to do this we can't afford to be vague.

KEEP IT SYMBOL

Emotions are extremely powerful – too powerful to be summed up by a single word. It's no use writing 'She felt so lonely, why hadn't he called?' As a six-letter word, lonely conveys nothing. In order to give the image strength, you have to find a concrete symbol that embodies what a character is feeling. This can be a metaphor: 'She threw the phone at the wall and fell to her knees, clawing at the carpet like a caged animal.' Alternatively, abstract emotions can be grounded through physical actions: 'She couldn't bear it, she wanted to give her heart to someone but he hadn't come. They never came. She folded her legs beneath her on the sofa and pressed her head into the upholstery. The pressure on her eyes felt like fingers, and she nuzzled harder, desperate for contact.'

Look at IDEA 5, *Shall I compare thee to a summer's day?*, for more advice on keeping the general personal.

Try another idea...

IDENTIFICATION PARADE

Metaphors and suggestive physical actions enable us to relate to and identify with abstract concepts, the indefinable becomes real, human, personal. I can't empathise with a character who simply feels 'lonely', but I can feel the pain and powerlessness of someone who craves physical contact. I can identify with the terrible need for company – and the inability to act on it – that drives someone to behave like a caged animal. These concrete images allow us to grapple with an abstract concept in a way that really evokes an emotional response; they create associations that enable a reader to comprehend an abstract thought on an intimate, personal level.

TOO MUCH OF A GOOD THING

It's easy to get carried away when trying to ground abstract terms – I do it all the time. Many metaphors can sound insincere and, even worse, clichéd. Use your instincts, and pick the metaphors and actions so evocative that they give you goosebumps. Whatever you do, don't force an image because you think it makes a work more poetical.

'Metaphors have a way of holding the most truth in the least space.'
ORSON SCOTT CARD, US novelist

Defining idea...

How did it go?

Q **I've been told that everything has symbolic value, but surely some things are just things? What about names, for example, are they symbolic?**

A *There's no such thing as a neutral name any more. Every name resonates with the imagery of its predecessors: whether it's Butch, Juliet, Ishmael, Oliver. Make sure you think hard about what this resonance says about your character, and whether it detracts from their believability. Also, have you given away too much in your character's name? Calling someone Cruella sort of gives the game away! Also think about whether you want people to read meaning into other aspects of your characters' lives: their jobs, their clothes and so on. Everything can have symbolic value.*

Q **I'm getting a bit blurry eyed with all this talk of emotions. Do all abstracts and metaphors have to work on an emotional level?**

A *Symbols don't just have to represent emotional concepts – they also work politically. Thousands of writers have used symbolic language to describe the politics of their homeland or the world in general, often to escape punishment, and often to subtly point out the links between the personal and the universal. Look at George Orwell's* Animal Farm *– ostensibly a story about the farmyard frolics of a group of animals, but in fact an explicit attack on totalitarianism.*

13

Who's the daddy: character or plot?

Like it or not, it's your characters that drive your work. Getting them right will make the difference between writing a masterpiece and an episode of *Days of Our Lives*.

Try to imagine 'Great Expectations' minus Pip. Or 'The Catcher in the Rye' sans Holden Caulfield, 'The Great Gatsby' without Gatsby, Emma without Emma, Harry Potter...you get the idea — if you don't get your characters right, your work won't work.

If Aristotle and E. M. Forster ever meet in the Great Beyond the encounter might just end in fisticuffs. These two had a great deal to say about the written work, but didn't always see eye to eye. Aristotle famously stated that plot was more important than character when it came to dramatic effect. Forster, on the other hand, claimed that in order for literature to work it has to be driven by its characters.

Here's an idea for you...

Pick a character you've been working on for a while and write several sketches placing them in unusual scenarios. Start off small: try several different seemingly mundane scenarios from your character's past, then pick something more dramatic, the kind of thing you'd find in a plot-based story – a nuclear explosion, an alien invasion, anarchy on the streets of the capital. Now place the same character in the action and see what happens.

Most writers side either with Aristotle in the red corner or back Forster in the blue. In other words, you either have organic characters in mind who are born into your fiction and left to develop much like real people, or you have the action in mind and carve your characters to fit. There are pros and cons to both approaches, but one of the similarities between the plot-driven story and the character-driven story is that in both cases the cast has to seem genuine.

NATURAL BIRTH...

Strong, well-developed characters can become so real in your mind that they drive the story. At one point in my own writing career I thought it impossible for the author to lose control, but while writing one novel I was amazed to find that the characters I had created didn't always want to follow my plan of action – like your own children finally learning to talk back. When they become 'autonomous' in this way, let them lead for a while. You might be pleasantly surprised where it takes you. Be warned, however, that when you let your characters off the leash they may wander errantly in circles and end up accomplishing nothing but boring a reader to tears.

...OR GENETICALLY ENGINEERED

For those of you thinking of approaching from the other side of the fence, a plot-driven narrative can be equally tricky. Writing your characters around a plot will almost always ensure that they do enough to sustain the reader's attention. The problem here, however, is whether they will do so realistically. Just like bespoke furniture, your characters can look a little artificial, as though they were constructed to fill a particular role and have no existence or history in your written world outside of this.

Read IDEA 6, *Blowing your trumpet*, for ways to subtly incorporate your own history and experience into your characters, creating more realistic personalities.

Try another idea…

ENTER THE REF

While literary fisticuffs are always entertaining, a healthy balance between plot and character is the path to success. Or, as Henry James put it, 'What is character but the determination of incident? What is incident but the illustration of character?' Plot is basically the result of human activities and adventures, and even if you don't know what's going to happen, your characters' actions will drive the narrative. In other words, if you've got a detailed enough understanding of your characters, the plot will evolve itself.

If, on the other hand, you're building your fiction around a plot, then this depth of character is still vital. Remember, even if you know what your plot will entail, your characters still don't. The incidents that occur in the course of the story will enable them to evolve and grow much like real people, and they must behave and respond like real people in those situations in order to seem real. If you don't have a grip of who your characters really are, then it doesn't matter how exciting the action, or how seamless the narrative: none of it will be convincing because the cast won't seem real.

'Plot is character and character plot.'
F. SCOTT FITZGERALD

Defining idea…

How did it go?

Q **I'm a big softie at heart and I'm not sure I want to put my characters in a dangerous situation. What should I be looking for in such a perilous task?**

A *The idea is to learn more about your characters by thinking about the way they'd act. Are they heroic or cowardly? Grounding a character in the reality of a more down-to-earth scene can help give a rounder picture of her, and make you think more carefully about the way she reacts to events.*

Q **I've heard people talk about round characters and flat characters. What's the difference?**

A *The terms were coined by E. M. Forster. Round characters are fully developed and comprehensively thought out; characters described in less detail, and who behave in stereotypical and predictable ways, are flat. By all means use flat characters for subsidiary roles (keeping secondary characters less developed stops them getting in the way of the main action), but always ensure your main characters are as well developed as possible.*

Q **Surely if my plot is exciting enough the characters just need to be props. Why should I take the time to question their motives?**

A *Go and wash your mouth out! Every character has to have a recognisable foundation of humanity. No matter who the reader is, they will know what it feels like to be scared, happy, angry, hopeful. If they can't see similar emotional responses in a character they won't empathise, and they'll just switch off.*

14

Born slippy

Creating realistic characters is as much a case of looking inwards as it is looking outwards. Learn to see what really makes people unique, mix these characteristics up and just wait for the newborns to emerge.

A successful writer is somebody with the ability to empathise with other human beings, somebody who can observe people in detail and then regurgitate this on to the page with every salient detail intact.

A successful writer can understand what motivates people, how they think, what their instincts are and what it is about their psychology that causes them to react the way they do. A successful writer can pick out the strange quirks of human behaviour and in doing so build a realistic portrait of how complex and surprising people actually are. Sounds daunting? Don't worry, it doesn't have to be: just look around you.

Here's an idea for you... **Pick a newspaper story, something juicy and scandalous from the tabloids. Try to imagine events from the viewpoint of one of the people involved. Begin by writing his interpretation of events. Try and capture his emotional response – in his own words. Now delve more deeply into the character: use the clues from what you've already written to find out his favourite book, his most treasured place, his wildest dream and biggest regret.**

YOUR BABIES

Fictional characters are one of life's great mysteries. They exist as nothing more than words and sentences, yet in the mind of a reader they can become more real than an actual human being. But where do these constructions come from? Some writers are lucky, and have a head full of characters that have bred there since childhood. Certainly the female protagonist from one of my novels existed in my mind for years before I ever put pen to paper, and by the time I started writing she seemed as real as any of my friends (which, I guess, is kind of embarrassing). She never actually existed as a person, but much of who she was came from real life – a mannerism here, a twitch there, a phobia from him, a kindness from her and so on. Ultimately, she was a patchwork of thoughts, looks, actions and speech that finally developed a life of its own in the melting pot of my brain.

BODY SNATCHERS

Most characters have their origins in the real world. This can be blatant – many writers have used people they know directly in their fiction – or it can be more subtle, like the example above. As a writer, it's up to you to remember the most fascinating aspects of a person's behaviour, to note what makes them tick. Watch your friends and families closely. Look for their idiosyncrasies, the driving force of their psychology, the past events that make them who they are; investigate what makes them nervous, or when they seem at their happiest. Use these characteristics as a repertory for your writing.

Take these observations, mix them up and filter them until characters emerge. Most of these will be 'ghosts', faint and grey, and most will disappear unwanted. But every now and again one will emerge that grips you, who seems almost real, and who takes up residence in your conscious mind. Don't ignore these squatters, investigate them, ask questions about their past, who they are, where they are going. The most potent characters will be those who attract your sympathy and attention, even those who start to really piss you off.

Sometimes people's possessions say more about them than the people do about themselves – look at IDEA 30, *Keeping up with the Joneses*, for ways to reveal information about characters through their surroundings.

Try another idea...

DON'T STOP THERE

While you will be able to observe people at their most natural in real life, characters can be found in every medium, from radio and television to books and comics. Look at what drives characters in the books you read and the films you watch. Make note of their physical and mental quirks, the way they hold themselves, the noise they make when they sneeze – everything! If you become particularly engaged with a character in a novel, ask yourself why. What is it about the way they are described that attracts your empathy? If you work this out, then you can encourage readers to empathise with your characters. By picking out the elements that make us human and attributing them to your character, readers will recognise themselves in the text and connect with it on a deeply emotional level.

'Writing is a socially acceptable form of schizophrenia.'
E. L. DOCTOROW, US novelist

Defining idea...

How did it go?

Q I've cast my friends, family and enemies in my work, but the annoying so-and-sos aren't acting the way I want them to! Why am I finding it so hard to force them to do things?

A Many writers have used real people in their writing, but it can cause difficulties. The most obvious is that your character may have to act differently to its real-life model, and when you are basing it on an actual person your imagination may be limited. If you know a person too intimately, then you may not be able to use him in your fiction as freely as you would an invented character. Use real people for inspiration but ensure you don't imitate them completely. Your characters should be unique, and under your control.

Q I'm having trouble climbing into other people's heads and discovering what makes them unique. Is there any way of, er, cheating?

A People don't always want to reveal their inner motivations, and if you know a few cagey people you might not be able to gather up too much information about their secret inner lives. Don't worry, try watching soap operas and television dramas – these programmes distil the most powerful and emotional moments in a person's life, providing you with a short cut to what makes them tick. Be careful, though, as soaps don't show people in every light, and in order to create fully rounded characters you need to be able to picture them in as diverse a range of situations as possible, not just the most dramatic ones.

15

You are what you own

Whether it's a tattered sombrero, a life-size Elvis doll or a 1970s Jaguar, what your characters own say everything about them. These tricks will help you bring them to life.

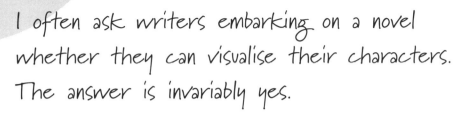

I often ask writers embarking on a novel whether they can visualise their characters. The answer is invariably yes.

I then ask 'So what do they carry in their pockets? How do they dance to their favourite song when nobody else is looking? What's their most treasured item of clothing? What kind of expression do they pull when faced with something that terrifies them?' The answer is invariably a series of ums and ahs. Whether you are writing poetry, prose or drama you must be able to visualise your characters clearly – not like that fuzzy memory of Aunt Mildred that hovers in the dusty corner of your mind.

PORTRAIT OF A LADY...

Or a gentleman, or a child, or a retired traffic warden, or any character that will be appearing in your writing. These portraits are what make literature sink or swim. If readers can't see a realistic person – somebody they believe they may bump into down the High Street – within a character, then they will find it hard to become

Here's an idea for you... **Having trouble visualising a new character? Write a list of twenty objects she might carry or wear. Don't think too deeply about this, just write down whatever comes to mind. Next, write a series of short sketches describing exactly how your character came by these items. Try to describe what the item means to her, and how she would feel if she lost it. You may never use these character sketches, but I guarantee they will give you – and your reader – a clearer sense of who your character is.**

engaged with your work. And for those of you who want to get stuck into stream of consciousness or fantastical narratives, listen up: you need to learn how to create realistic characters before you can bend the rules. Even Picasso was a master of the life drawing before he embarked on cubism.

PLAYING GOD

I won't lie to you – creating characters with a realistic depth of feeling and a believable, three-dimensional existence on the page is extremely difficult. It's like playing god. We conjure these 'people' from nothing and give them life, tell them what to wear, how to act. But like any good deity we also have to give them free will, otherwise they can appear staged, or lifeless. But there are tricks to making this complicated process much easier.

POCKET PICKING

When starting to create your characters, keep the phrase 'you are what you own' in the forefront of your mind. Of course we are all more than the sum of our possessions, but the items that people wear or carry with them can reveal a great deal about who they are – and can be used to subtly convey information about them in your written work. Think about somebody dear to you, picture him in your head. What does she carry in her pockets (or her handbag) at all times? An inhaler, a lucky rubber band, a photograph of a child, a pocket watch, a knife, the ear of an enemy killed in battle (unlikely, but you may have some odd friends)?

Take a detailed look at IDEA 7, _Digging the dirt_, for advice on making your characters, and their jobs, seem realistic.

Try another idea...

When we remember people we don't always recall snippets of information like this, but these tiny details are vital for creating a character that leaps off the page into the reader's consciousness. A character's possessions and clothes are an extension of their personality; by paying close attention to which of these details you reveal, you can control how readers see and engage with your characters.

A person's items can reveal an element of their personality that is not directly evident – maybe an old lady is carrying the knife. They might give insights into a character's hidden emotional depths – a young man who gives no clues as to how he is feeling could panic at the thought of losing a pocket watch given to him by his father. Or they can create a sense of mystery or surprise that adds to a character's depth – take the photograph of the child. Is she still alive? Was she kidnapped/killed/abducted by aliens? Even when the details aren't directly relevant to the plot, being able to fine-tune the image of your characters on the page will allow them to emerge as individuals, not merely clusters of words.

'*We first make our habits, then our habits make us.*'
JOHN DRYDEN

Defining idea...

How did
it go?

Q **I'd make a pretty hopeless Frankenstein. Every time I try and build up a character I put the parts together wrong, and end up with a monster. Can this exercise help create new characters?**

A *Sure. If you're having trouble imagining a character for your work, then write a list of twenty items – clothing and/or personal effects. Then try to imagine what kind of person would wear/carry these.*

Q **I've already decided on every aspect of my character's appearance and personality. Is there any point in me trying this exercise?**

A *Yes! You can still write a list of possessions for characters in a book you have already drafted, especially if you feel they lack realism or depth. You may not even use items in the list, but simply by imagining your character's emotional engagement or interaction with an object you will learn more about them, and uncover secrets about their personality you'd never even considered before.*

Q **I picked twenty objects but they are all things that belong to me, and now my character seems to be a mirror image. Am I unhealthily vain or is this OK?**

A *The trick with this exercise is to think of objects that are strange and unfamiliar to you. Not things that you own. If you do want to use familiar objects, however, then it is vital to see them through somebody else's eyes. What may seem like a common, everyday object to you may have intense emotional significance to somebody else.*

16

Say what?

There's little worse than characters what don't speak proper – believable dialogue is the first step to a believable world, and is a great way to get to know who your characters really are...

Dialogue can seem deceptively easy. After all, it's just a selection of people speaking to one another, right?

If you look at some of Hemingway's early short fiction you can see how effective a dialogue-based story can be. There is very little actual action, just a great deal of talking. But try and write a similar piece and you may run into difficulties making the speech realistic and relevant.

SPEAK ONLY WHEN SPOKEN TO

The secret of writing effective dialogue in your fiction is not to emulate real speech, but to give the impression of real speech. Think about the last conversation you had. It may have seemed short, but imagine having to transcribe it onto the page. Chances are it would seem ridiculously long-winded, tautological and quite boring to a reader, especially one who doesn't know you. Ironically, this 'real speech' would appear artificial in a work of fiction because the conventions for writing dialogue

Here's an idea for you... **Tape record two or more people in conversation, in any situation, and then transcribe it. Next, rewrite the dialogue as though for your own story, editing it and adding action and attributive verbs. Look at what changes you make, and how much you need to prune, before it looks 'realistic' on the page.**

are different to those that govern everyday conversation. It may seem odd at first, but keep your dialogue short and to the point, and don't hold back when you're editing. The more you prune (even if it seems unusually to the point), the smoother the ride.

Real speech is forever punctuated by hesitations, interruptions, circumlocutions, evasions and the odd sneezing fit. These attributes can come in handy for plot and characterisation ('Well,' he hesitated, looking away, 'I didn't steal them') but don't include them in every piece of dialogue. Readers look for the meaning in every interaction, every spoken word, so only include interruptions when they mean something. Although nobody speaks perfectly all the time, dialogue full of wheezes, pauses and fumblings won't win any admirers.

READ BETWEEN THE LINES

How many times have you said something and meant something else, or mumbled a few words that you hoped would mean so much more? Very often, real speech only hints at the powerful undercurrents of meaning that lie beneath, and when writing it's vital to get these subtexts right if you want to convey psychological depth and realism. A married woman screaming 'I'm sick of this house, I want to move on' could obliquely be asking for a divorce, not just complaining about the décor.

'...AND ANOTHER THING,' HE MUTTERED MOODILY

My partner often says to me 'It's not what you said, it's the way you said it.' While it's easy to change the tone or style of your speech in real life, it's impossible to do so on paper without a few clues. If a woman says to a man 'I love you', it can be difficult to ascertain exactly how she feels. You can often clarify the dialogue by adding an action: '"I love you," she said, tenderly squeezing his hand.' Or you can completely change the meaning: '"I love you," she hissed, glancing warily at the knife.' Physical actions like these can help ground the speech in the scene, making it appear more realistic, and can also be used to help develop your characters.

See IDEA 17, *Accent marks*, for help on what to do if your character starts speaking with an accent.

Try another idea...

ONE LAST THING

Speech doesn't always have to be out loud. While direct speech – spoken audibly from one character to another – is highly effective, indirect (or reported) speech can also work: 'She told Jamie she loved him, that she always would.' Alternatively, interior monologues can be used to convey unspoken speech: '"I love you," she thought, "I only wish I could tell you."' Interior speech can be extremely useful, providing a glimpse in to the character's true state of mind, but use with caution, as too much and readers may think you're being lazy.

'The dialogue is generally the most agreeable part of a novel, but only so long as it tends in some way to the telling of the main story.'
ANTHONY TROLLOPE

Defining idea...

How did
it go?

Q   I've tried your suggestions, but are there any techniques for adding meaning to speech other than physical action?

A   *Yes. You can add an abstract explanation to give meaning to the spoken word: '"I love you," she said. This time, she really meant it.' Be wary, though, as too much of this and your work can seem insincere.*

Q   I'm having terrible flashbacks of my English teacher drumming out the rules for laying out speech. Was he right?

A   *Many writers argue against restricting text with grammatical rules, and have broken with tradition in the way they lay out their dialogue. Convention states that speech should be demarcated by single speech marks, that a new paragraph should be used each time a different character speaks, and that actions associated with the speaker when they are talking are included in the same paragraph. Off the record, however, you can lay out your dialogue how you like – just make sure your readers know when somebody is speaking, otherwise it could get messy.*

Q   When I was a kid I used 'he said/she said' with every piece of speech. Should I follow suit as an adult?

A   *You don't need to attribute every piece of speech with a 'he said/she said', but if there are lots of people talking, or the dialogue is frequently switching back and forth between characters, then it's useful to provide occasional markers. It's far better to give each character such a distinctive way of speaking that the reader always knows who is talking, supporting this with the odd indicator. And go easy on the attributive verbs (postulated, lied, suggested, joked, screamed and so on): use these only when you really need to.*

17

Accent marks

You may have the most realistically depicted characters in literary history, but if they fall to pieces as soon as they open their mouth then nobody is going to take them seriously. Fear not, your voice coach has arrived...

Eh up me duck, g'day, och aye the noo, well Yakky Da Gor Blimey an' ting pardners. No, it's not an impressionist on speed, it's a worst-case example of what can happen if you mess up your dialect.

Your character's voice is a large part of how credible he appears on the page, so it's vital to hit the spot. Every character will have different speech patterns that in turn will vary depending on their physical and emotional state. By the end of your text, readers should be able to recognise a speaker by her speech. This means much more than highlighting an accent every now and again, but the accent is a good place to start.

Where is your character from? Up north? Down south? Australia, America, Mongolia? Emphasizing an accent is hard (get it wrong and you end up with Officer

Here's an idea for you...

Get hold of a recording of people talking with an accent or in a dialect. Try to ascertain what makes it different from your own way of speaking, then work out how it would look when transcribed on paper. Write the words as they sound, even if they look ridiculous. Experiment by allowing your character to speak in a full regional accent, or just sneak in the odd word or two to their speech to give it the appearance of an accent. It may take a while, but you'll eventually find the right balance between plain speech and dialect.

Crabtree from '*Allo 'Allo* – in fact it's incredible how often a phoney accent is used to humorous effect). You have to decide from the start how much you want to use it in your writing, and remember to stay consistent.

STAYING SUBTLE

Most commonly, an accent is subtly hinted at by the narrator – 'his soft Irish lilt' – and contributed to with the occasional reminder in the character's speech. In extreme cases, however, entire novels can be written in dialect – Irvine Welsh wrote almost all of *Trainspotting* in 'Scottish' (which some consider to be another language entirely). Be very careful if you are following suit. Dialect can be extremely difficult to convey on the page in a way that readers will appreciate, and this is less to do with the vernacular than the spelling. Readers left to ponder over the pronunciation or interpretation of a word will be bound up in your story's literary construction, not its meaning, and will quickly grow impatient.

Stick to the light touches. If your readers know your character has an accent, then the odd idiosyncratic spelling or misspelled word will be enough to remind them. Keep in mind that you're trying to give the impression of speech, not to replicate it – making it easy for the reader should come before verbal verisimilitude.

AND WHAT ABOUT NARRATORS?

If you've elected to write with a first-person narrative style, then be warned – if your character speaks with a discernible accent then

For more ideas about making your dialogue realistic, read IDEA 16, Say what!?

Try another idea...

you may have to use it throughout. Not always, though, as you could limit the accent to the character's speech, not his narration. Third-person narratives allow a greater distinction between the narrative voice and the character's speech, but it's still worth taking care. You need to keep a mental note of how your characters talk, or any interjections from them may seem out of place.

MIRACLE CURES

But realistic speech is about more than just an accent. Are there any figures of speech commonly used in the character's home town? Or, if it is a historical novel, are your characters using phrases or sayings that haven't been coined yet? It's worth spending the time researching the location or period you've chosen for your work, as even the smallest mistake may prove to be a hefty embarrassment. Away from cultural, historical and geographical specifics, consider your character's own way of speaking. Do they have any impediments, or any verbal idiosyncrasies that separate them from the crowd? If so, make sure they don't miraculously heal midway through the text (I know you're not an idiot, but you'd be surprised how many times I've seen it happen).

'I was just pissing by and have good nose – the troon has been bummed by the RAF.'
OFFICER CRABTREE, *'Allo, 'Allo*

Defining idea...

How did it go?

Q **I'm setting my work in a foreign country. Should I don my old school uniform, make up a pack lunch and get reacquainted with Madame Brassiére?**

A *Well, you don't have to learn Spanish to be able to set your book in Spain. Nor do you want to write every piece of dialogue with a dialect. If two foreign characters are talking to one another, write in plain English, as they would be able to understand each other perfectly. If you like, throw in the odd recognisable foreign word just to remind the reader where the scene is set.*

Q **Dialect is one thing, but do you reckon I could get away with inventing an entire language for my book, and using words that don't actually exist?**

A *You don't need me to tell you that if you write a text in a language unique to you, then nobody else will be able to read it. But this doesn't mean you can't use words from a 'new' language every now and again. Look at the use of Nadsat in Anthony Burges's* A Clockwork Orange. *It adds to, rather than detracts from, the atmosphere of alienation and violence. And don't forget Tolkien. He spent decades working on the various languages for* The Lord of the Rings, *but included translations to ensure nobody got lost.*

18

There may be trouble ahead

The most memorable fictional characters all face up to some kind of conflict – from global threats to personal dilemmas – so learn to treat 'em mean if you want to keep the readers keen.

Practically all characters in fiction are driven by the conflicts they face and the choices they make.

We're not just talking adventure novels and horror tales. Conflict is at the heart of all good writing, it's what drives it forwards. Novels, screenplays and poems are all journeys undertaken by their main characters. This journey forces them to make choices, many of them extremely difficult, and through these pressurised decisions your characters show their true colours.

It's vital to know your characters intimately when you are writing, otherwise the way they face up to conflict may seem unrealistic or insincere, and they won't develop. It doesn't matter if your characters make wrong decisions, only that their choices are realistic and human. It's this lack of predictability, the anticipation and surprise of expectation and result, which keeps the readers hooked.

Here's an idea for you...

Start to plan out a history for each of your main characters. Use events from your own past, or steal anecdotes from the people you know. Books, films and television can also be a valuable resource, as can the 'real-life story' articles in weekly magazines. I can guarantee that once you've got a better idea of your characters' history, you'll have a much more vivid sense of who they are, how they see the world and how they react to conflict.

LEGITIMATE ABUSE

You may already have a plot in mind, and be ready to throw your characters into a melting pot of conflict and difficulty. But even if you haven't yet settled on a story, or are waiting to see where your characters will lead, it's a good idea to work out where the conflict lies. All good characters are plagued by an internal conflict (and remember, even the smallest, most domestic conflict can seem immense in the eyes of whoever is suffering it). You'll probably find that the characters you have in mind – even if they are only outlines – are troubled in some way. Without conflict, how can your character even have a view of the world?

HISTORY LESSONS

Your characters must have a history. Do you know the key events of their past, the ones that made them who they are (the bullying at school, the betrayal of or by a loved one, the death of a parent, the birth of a child)?

The conflicts your characters will face may well be something to do with an event from the past, and having a clear idea of what your character has already endured and experienced will help you generate realistic scenarios. Even if you're focusing on plot, your characters' reactions to events will be largely determined by the events of their past, so it's vital to look back as well as forwards. Remember, it's how your characters deal with the world that makes writing interesting, so give them motivations and reasons for acting the way they do in the

Learn more about researching pasts and professions in IDEA 7, *Digging the dirt.*

Try another idea...

face of adversity. You might not use any of this 'research' verbatim in your writing, but time spent investigating your characters' pasts will give you a much clearer idea of who they are, and enable you to keep their behaviour consistent throughout.

YOUR TRUE COLOURS SHINING THROUGH

As your characters face up to the pressures of the story, they will change. This may be planned (the nerdy cinema usher becomes the hero during an alien invasion, perhaps), or it may come as a surprise. Don't be shocked if your characters respond to a difficulty in a way you hadn't expected – when faced with a conflict on the page they may just take action in their own way. The more you know about their past, the greater the sense of freedom and motivation the characters will have, and the more realistic their response. A poorly thought out character will always obey convention, or will defy expectation but in a way nobody will believe. In other words, he will become stereotypical. A character with depth and with a past, however, will surprise you and delight the reader by revealing herself in a new light.

'Often I'll find clues to where the story might go by figuring out where the characters would rather not go.'
DOUG LAWSON, US writer

Defining idea...

How did it go?

Q **I know who my characters are, and I want to think of conflicts for them, but I'm just too nice. Do I have to upset their world?**

A *Just remember that characters don't have to be heroic to be exciting, and the conflicts they face don't have to be monumental. Emma Bovary was a bored housewife, yet her story is world famous.*

Q **Do I really have to think of a history for my characters? I'm writing a plot-based text (set around the apocalypse, incidentally, conflict guaranteed!). Surely my characters' past is irrelevant. Right?**

A *The apocalypse, eh? Can I offer you (gratis)* The Morning After *as a working title? Seriously, though, if you don't have a clear idea of who the characters are, then their actions will appear false to a reader. If your characters do heroic (or cowardly) things, you need to give the reader an indication why.*

Q **OK, point taken. So my characters must have some conflict in their lives. But how do I get to the bottom of this?**

A *Try asking your characters some of the following questions: do they live alone? When and why did they leave home? Are they successful, financially, romantically? What kind of jobs have they had? Which members of their family have died? What was their school-life like? When did they first discover their sexuality? How does what they want from life now differ from what they wanted as a child, and how do they feel about this change? Don't just make this up – ask them.*

19

It's alive!

So, you know your characters inside out, you can picture them in your head, you can smell their perfume, and you know exactly what drives them to act. Now you just have to convey all of this on the page...

Being at one with your characters is only the beginning. Bringing them alive in a text in a way that readers will get to grips with is an entirely different problem.

When reading, you automatically build up a physical description of a character in your mind's eye. Take 'the young man entered the bar'. You most probably have an image of a young man, albeit a very fuzzy one. But every reader will probably be picturing a different person, and it's up to you as a writer to ensure they pick up on the important points.

Victorian novels used to devote hundreds, sometimes thousands, of words to describing a character, but these days that isn't always necessary. Think carefully about how you want readers to see a character. You can say a great deal about them in a little space: 'The young man, decked in baggy blue jeans and a chequered, double-stitched jacket worn lightly over a tucked-in blue t-shirt, entered the bar.'

Here's an idea for you...

Pick a character that you can imagine clearly, one that you've been working on for a while. Now write a sketch, and use this to practise balancing the various means of conveying characters – physical description, interjection, action, association, soliloquy, speech, and the thoughts and comments of an observer – until the sketch flows smoothly. Try to imagine what a reader wants to be told or shown, and what can be left to the imagination. Try some different genres – horror, romance, sci-fi, western – to see whether the way you describe your character varies.

AND ACTION!

But you can also risk boring a reader with clumsy description – do we need to know exactly what he is wearing? Description is largely passive, so keep it as tight as possible: 'The young man entered the bar, his jacket clutched against the blood stains on his shirt.'

THE AUTHOR'S COMMENT

Whilst description is a potent means of making a character stand out on the page, it is sometimes necessary for a novelist to interject. 'He could barely see, but beneath the drooping lids his eyes still burned, a look of pure hatred the barman would never forget.' This is obviously the narrator's statement, but it helps add depth and mystery to the scene. Is the barman responsible for the young man's injuries?

Physical action is always more effective than passive description. It can say more than any interjection by the author, and in a much more involved way. 'He staggered forwards, slipping on the crimson pool that had formed beneath his bare feet. There was an audible intake of breathe from around the room as he pulled the gun from his waistband, pointing it unsteadily in the direction of the bar.'

ASSOCIATION

This more subtle form of description leaves the interpretation to the reader, but can be much more effective than a simple list of physical attributes. 'Everybody could see the silver crucifix coiled around the barrel, and tucked beneath it, creased so many times it was barely recognisable, the photo of his baby daughter.' These small details in the scene provide hints to the character's motives and psychology. They are descriptive, but they also suggest a little more: the crucifix could signify the man's honourable motives, the photo justifies the revenge. Association can be reversed, however, so don't always use it conventionally.

Check out IDEA 15, *You are what you own*, to learn more about physical description, and look at IDEA 16, *Say what?*, for techniques to improve speech.

Try another idea...

ARE YOU TALKING TO ME?

Another means of putting your character across on the page is by allowing readers access to their thoughts. These interior monologues provide information that cannot be ascertained by description or action. 'This was it, he thought, trying to make sense of his blurred vision, trying to see past the pain, I'm finally going to kill him. This is for you, Sara.' Likewise, actual speech can reveal just as much about your character. '"Time's up Frost," he muttered, centring the gun's sights on the motionless shape behind the bar, "It's all over. You should have stayed the hell away from my family."'

Finally, other people's thoughts or speech can be used to bring your character to life, adding another dimension to their behaviour. 'Frost clamped his hands on the worn wood of the

'No tears in the writer, no tears in the reader. No surprise in the writer, no surprise in the reader.'
ROBERT FROST

Defining idea...

85

bar and faced the wounded man. Payne looked as though he'd been run through a mangle then fed to the dogs – he could barely stand up. '"Payne," he scowled, raising his arms in defence, "You know it wasn't me that killed your kids. It was you, Payne. You did it yourself."'

How did it go?

Q **I'm trying to use association, but it's ending up cheesier than a Parisien fromagerie. Are there any clever ways to employ the technique?**

A *We associate certain actions and objects with various types of people. A person toying with a rosary we assume to be a devout Catholic, a man in a balaclava we see as a terrorist. But too much of this and characters simply become stereotypical. In the main example above, showing Payne with a crucifix around his gun could represent honourable motives, but it could also be the opposite of this: perhaps he thinks that an emblem of god will justify a series of murders, however horrific or random.*

Q **I've had a hard day at work and don't feel like juggling the different techniques listed here. Can't I just tell readers what happens in a scene using description?**

A *You could, but the end result would resemble a newspaper report, not a piece of fiction. Description is passive, and the easiest way to get something across. Because of this, readers will soon grow tired of being told what's going on in such a lifeless fashion. Instead, vary the above techniques to show what happens, keeping up the pace and ensuring that readers remain engaged.*

20

Fast and furious

Film characters are only on screen for a couple of hours, so they have to move fast. Use these tried and tested methods for getting the audience on your side as soon as the curtains open.

The intense focus of the camera can create a unique level of emotional realism and identification. How is this instant empathy achieved? Listen up...

On the big screen, it may seem like the plot's the most important thing, but all good films are character driven. Even if the movie's about the end of the world, it's an audience's responses to the characters that determine its success.

I NEED A HERO

Films usually have a single protagonist: the character your audience focuses on, empathises with and follows throughout the story. This 'hero/ine' is the force that drives the plot, the engine that initiates the action. Because of this, you should know them back to front – as well as a novelist knows her characters. If an actor, producer or director asks you why a character does or says something, you have to have a plausible answer.

Here's an idea for you...

Your main character must be transformed, gradually, during the course of the film. It's your job as a writer to make the audience hungry to know why a character acts, what drives them. Ask yourself these questions. What does the character want or desire and why do they want it (including the subconscious reasons)? What lengths will they go to in order to get it? What could they lose if they fail (this has to be significant – if there's no risk, there's no story)?

In order to make your protagonist believable, ensure that he has three recognisable dimensions, each of which feeds into the others. The first of these is action: a character has to behave in a believable way, both physically and psychologically. Then there are emotions: screenplays are emotions dramatised in the form of conflict. Add credibility to your characters by focusing on their emotional make-up and their emotional actions. Lastly, your characters have to have a recognisable personality: a combination of integrated interior beliefs (aspirations, attitudes, prejudices, etc.)

If any of these dimensions are missing, your characters will appear flat. All of these facets reveal themselves to a writer when you are 'investigating' a character's past – the better you know your characters, the more realistic their behaviour will seem, and the more people will identify with them.

SYMPATHY FOR THE DEVIL

The most important thing to remember when thinking about your protagonist is that you have to encourage the audience to empathise and like him as quickly as possible. If you get the audience on your side, if you can get viewers to feel engaged with a character near the beginning, they'll watch to the end of the film. The brief list that follows shows some ways of achieving this.

- Likeability: if a character is introduced as being likeable, audiences will empathise with whatever happens to her.

See IDEA 36, *All good things come in threes*, for a closer look at a screenplay's structure.

Try another idea...

- Sympathy: if your protagonist is an undeserved victim of something early on, the audience will want to see him redeemed.

- Danger: the audience will identify with a character they are worried about, whether the danger is mortal or simply loss of face.

- Inequality: if a character is downtrodden, vulnerable or oppressed, an audience will sympathise with him.

- Curiosity: if a character is mysterious, audiences will want to know more, even if it's a character they don't like – though always remember to give a dislikeable character at least one redeeming feature.

And if you're looking for something a little more subtle, try some of the following. Empathy: a mix of sympathy, danger and likeability – powerful, but difficult to create. A character has to be fairly ordinary for an audience to empathise. Familiarity: using a recognisable setting or giving a character familiar behavioural traits (burning his shirt when ironing, losing her keys, etc.) will help the audience identify. Admiration: if an audience admires a character (not necessarily in a likeable way), they will keep watching. Power: we're all fascinated by it – give a character power and an audience will be strangely entranced.

'People go to the cinema to see themselves on the screen.'
MICHAEL CAINE

Defining idea...

How did
it go?

Q **OK, I've pinned down my main character, but surely I don't have to go to the same lengths for my support characters. Just how important are they anyway?**

A *Very. If your support cast isn't rounded and believable your protagonists risk losing their on-screen strength. Having a well-developed support cast will enable you to add depth to main characters by allowing them to reveal themselves in believable and interesting ways.*

Q **What about a duffer's guide to supporting characters?**

A *First up is the bad guy, the antagonist, the nemesis – the character who tries to prevent the protagonist reaching her goal. Good villains always make good drama (and a bad guy doesn't have to be human – it can be an animal, a monster, a volcano). Next up, the love interest: the object of your protagonist's romantic or sexual desire and often the goal at the end of the story. Always make sure that your audience falls in love with your love interest too. Lastly there's the mirror character, the character who supports the heroine's goals or who's in the same boat. The mirror character is used to reveal the main character in more depth.*

Q **And one more question: just how religiously should I stick to these categories?**

A *Remember, every single person, no matter how archetypal they seem, is in a constant flux, driven by their personality. If you've really thought out your characters their humanity will show. Because of this, support characters can often 'shapeshift', switching from a mirror to a love interest, a love interest to a villain, a villain to a mirror and so on – how often has the 'best friend' turned out to be the evil mastermind? Use the four character types as a starting point but always remember to keep them as real as possible.*

21

Playing god

Every piece of writing has to have a viewpoint. Somebody, or something, has to tell the story, and the choice has profound implications for the way a reader engages with your text.

The point of view you select is crucial. It's the window to your literary world, and if it's pointing in the wrong direction nobody's going to want to look through it.

Let's start off with the holiest perspective: the god's eye view. It's one of the great advantages of being a writer: you can create a world all of your own and assume absolute, godlike power over it. The third-person narrator can be everywhere, seeing everything, an omniscient voyeur peering deep inside the mind of any character and poring over their most intimate thoughts. Like a giant laboratory assistant, this narrative voice selects the most salient details from the lives of its lab rats and lays them out for inspection. Just look at Dickens for excellent examples of the god's eye view at work.

Here's an idea for you... **Take a piece of writing you have already penned – it doesn't have to be long, anywhere between 200 and 500 words – or write a fresh piece using a couple of your characters. Next, write it again using a different perspective, then again, with yet another. Which perspective best conveys what you're trying to say, and which allows the most empathy with the characters on the page?**

ALL SEEING, ALL KNOWING – AND LOST

But don't get too carried away, your almightyship. The most problematic disadvantage to the omniscient third person is a lack of engagement with the world it's describing. You can be so busy hovering over the landscape, picking out details, dropping in and out of people heads, or floating through houses like an errant spirit that you lose focus, and forget to engage with the characters. In the same way, a narrator faced with such an enormous landscape, and so much scope, confronts a real nightmare trying to decide which things matter to a reader, and which things don't. Like a kid in a candy store, you don't always know what to go for first.

YES, PROFESSOR

Back in the early days of the novel, authors often favoured an omniscient third-person approach because it allowed them to state their mind whenever they felt it necessary. This didactic, intrusive style sometimes worked – take the learned intrusions of George Eliot and the cosy asides from Jane Austen. But the presence of a third-person narrator who offers an opinion on everything that is happening can become a bore. In certain texts it's OK to venture off on an erudite digression, but don't lecture people on how they should read your work. It's far better to take a subtle approach and gently steer people towards your way of thinking. You can push readers in the right direction with clever narration and characterisation, but you can't boss them around.

HOW IRONIC!

One clever way of getting round this is to use your third-person narrator ironically. Yes, it's that word we all hated at school, but it's a great method for subtly adding opinion and humour to your work. The key thing to remember is that the best irony is implicit, and only hinted at. If you start explaining why it's ironic, it stops being clever and just becomes annoying.

To cut a long story short, irony occurs when there's a discrepancy between what a character or narrator thinks is true and what is really true. This can be with dialogue: '"I never eat more than one dish for lunch," she muttered proudly as she finished her third course'; with beliefs: 'She stepped confidently into the alley. Nobody would attack a little old lady, she thought, especially in the middle of Glasgow'; with expectations and results: 'Saddam laughed to himself – the Americans would never invade Iraq'; or with appearance and reality: 'He stepped forwards. The old rope bridge looked perfectly safe'. These are pretty obtuse examples, but it shows how irony can be used to make a point without rubbing your opinions in a reader's face.

Learn about other forms of viewpoint in IDEAS 22, 23 and 24, and pick up pointers to stop your plot spiralling out of control in IDEA 34, *Every which way but loose.*

Try another idea...

'*The choice of the point of view from which the story is told is arguably the most important single decision that the novelist has to make, for it fundamentally affects the way readers will respond, emotionally and morally, to the fictional characters and their actions.*'
DAVID LODGE

Defining idea...

93

How did it go?

Q **I'm trying out different narrative styles but how can I rein in my omniscient narrator? It wants to talk about everything, and at this rate my novel is going to be 10,000 pages long!**

A *And the chances are that nobody will want to read it. So you've discovered that playing god can be a bit of a headache? You're faced with too much choice about what to write about, what to include? I won't lie – it takes an enormous amount of practice and an even greater amount of editing to perfect this narrative style. It also helps if you know your story inside out before you start writing. But don't give in, eventually you'll find the right balance.*

Q **I've tried all your narrative suggestions and now I just don't know which to go with. Is there a quick way of finding out for sure which viewpoint works best?**

A *The only way of knowing for sure is to try different angles and different styles of narration. Listen to your inner voice: chances are you already have a strong intuition about which narrative style to use, especially if you have a feel for your central character. Just keep writing. If it feels wrong, try something else.*

22

Variations on a theme

Just because you want to use a third-person narrator in your writing doesn't mean he/she/it has to be omniscient. The third-person limited could be just the compromise you're looking for.

OK, so you want to use a third-person narrative style, but don't want to play god – after all, know-it-alls can be such a bore!

You want to embody your narrator somehow without making it the main character. You want to tell the story from a personal viewpoint, but you also want to be able to peek up and over the shoulders of your characters every now and again to see what lies ahead. Well, you may be surprised to know that you can have your cake and eat it – by using the third-person limited.

LIMITED BY NAME ONLY

A third-person narrator doesn't have to have god-like abilities, and doesn't need to intrude on the action. Its omniscience can be limited so that it only sees the world from one particular viewpoint, from close behind one particular character. This way, the narrator becomes more intimately associated with the action, and a greater sense of mystery can be preserved. The narrator is still distinct from the characters,

Here's an idea for you... **Find an extract from a novel, or a poem, written in the first person, one that's rich in emotion and personality. Now rewrite it in the third-person limited. Try to keep the same sense of emotional intensity and idiosyncrasy. What are the main differences between the original and your rewrite? Now select an extract with an omniscient third-person narrator. Pick a character from the piece and write events from his/her point of view using the third-person limited. This exercise will help you see how different the techniques are from one another, and the advantages and disadvantages of each.**

but is now in the same boat, and in just as much danger of being blindsided.

CHOICES, CHOICES, CHOICES

It is important, when deciding to use the third-person limited, to determine from the start just how limited the narrator is going to be. At its most restrained, the third person will only be able to see through the eyes of a single character: 'He could see her expression turn as hard as steel, but what she was thinking?' But you may decide to give your narrator more power and let it view things even when nobody is present: 'He sauntered through the graveyard gates. "I'm such a lucky guy," he thought to himself. Behind him, out of sight, the zombie pulled itself free of the grave.' Here, your narrator is bordering on the omniscient, but you have more freedom to hold things back.

The narrator may be able to share information with the reader that the character does not know – 'She looked at the sweat forming on her husband's brow and felt sorry for him. Her reaction would have been different if she'd seen the waitress leaping from the window seconds before she burst through the door.' Or it may only be able to witness what the protagonist is aware of: 'She threw open the door. Her husband stood there, dripping sweat. Could she smell perfume? A trail of scent that seemed to linger around the open window.' With even more insight, the narrator may be able to see from the viewpoint of several main characters, perhaps a different one in each chapter.

NO PEEKING

Try to stay consistent. Readers need to know exactly what, or who, is telling the story. If you write half a story, or worse, half a novel, with the narrator firmly rooted in the mind of a single character, then abruptly allow it to see into the future to an event that will shape that character's life, it's more than likely that a reader's mental alarm bells will start ringing. This may make them more aware of the literary construction than the events in progress; or worse, they may feel so cheated that they throw the text aside. Likewise, readers used to a narrator who has let them access all areas may become frustrated at the sudden use of blinkers.

STREAM OF CONSCIOUSNESS

You've probably heard this phrase bandied about in relation to James Joyce and Virginia Woolf, but what does it mean? It was actually coined by Henry James' brother William (rather tight, these literary circles) to describe the random flow of impressions through a character's mind. But why not use first person to delve into a person's mind? You can, but once you are in, there's no coming out. By using a third-person narrator you can literally dip your finger in the torrential stream of one

Try another idea...

Check out what happens when you give a third-person narrator divine powers in IDEA 21, *Playing god.*

Defining idea...

'It seems to me important that you should always love the inner experience of the story, and the characters in it, experiencing along with them; rather than using them illustratively.'
MALCOLM BRADBURY

character's thoughts, then do the same to another's. It can end up resembling a complicated jumble of phrases (*Ulysses*, anyone?), but by including a pattern, however slight, it can become extremely powerful. Look at Michael Cunningham's *The Hours* for a recent example of how to make it work.

How did it go?

Q   I'm trying the exercise above but my partner keeps moaning that there's no real difference between the third-person limited and the first person. Can you tell him so he'll pipe down?

A   *The two styles are very similar. With the first person, though, it's the character who's talking. With the third-person limited, it's a separate narrator, although they are so entwined in the character's thoughts they are practically inseparable. With the third-person limited you can move outside your character if you want to describe their responses or what they look like – something that's difficult to pull off with a first-person viewpoint.*

Q   Does the third-person limited have to be written in standard English, or can I make it more idiosyncratic?

A   *Generally speaking, a limited third-person narrator uses fairly standard English. In other words, no accent or dialect is used. This isn't a rule, however, and if you want to enhance third-person limited with a dialect it can often radically change the way a piece is read.*

23

What are you looking at?

It's rare, but when used effectively second-person narration can knock the reader's socks off.

Anybody who read Fighting Fantasy books when they were younger will know the second-person narrative style intimately: 'You enter the cavern and see a werewolf dead ahead. What will you do?'

This viewpoint is something of an outsider in narrative theory, but when used well it can have a profound effect on your reader. It is 'you' at the centre of things, 'you' who is now implicated in the story, for better or for worse. Of course, the second person can also be used to express intimacy and companionship, as this book hopefully demonstrates!

COME CLOSER, LET ME WHISPER

Self-help books aside, you need a good reason to use second-person narrative style in your work. Think about what you are trying to achieve – do you want the reader to feel like a character? Do you want to boss them around, to force them into a

Here's an idea for you... **Think of a scary or highly passionate scenario: a character walking alone on a deserted road at night after their car has broken down, or someone who feels they have bitterly disappointed their parents. Now write a poem or short prose sketch using the second person, and really try and get across the feeling of isolation.**

certain frame of thought? Do you want to convey the sense of a shared, intimate experience? Or do you want to make the reader complicit in whatever is going on in the text? One striking novel that uses the second person for precisely this last effect is Iain Banks' *Complicity*. Several of the chapters involve 'you' as the protagonist. Although it's not immediately clear what you are doing, you soon realise that 'you' are a serial killer, and you're forced to witness – commit, even – several horrific murders from a very intimate, and unsettling, viewpoint.

This feels like you're behind the eyes of a killer. Whereas with a more conventional form of narrative you could distance yourself from the events, here you literally are complicit with them. Like it or not, you become the character and have to sit with a puppet-like empathy as you maraud your way through your victims. On a less disturbing level, the second person works to make reading the text as strange an experience as possible. People aren't generally used to being addressed in a work of fiction. By doing so, you are creating an intimate bond with each reader, allowing them to take the front seat in your imaginary world. Used well, and your work will really stand out from the crowd. Used without good reason, though, or written sloppily and all it will do is confuse and alienate people.

YES YOU, DEAR READER

Writing an entire text in the second person is an ambitious, and some might say foolhardy, undertaking, but there's nothing to stop you addressing the reader every now and again. Back in the good old days when the novel was a relatively new phenomenon, narrators often made conversational asides to the reader. And whilst not as common today, the narrator can still throw in an occasional comment or two directed at 'you', just to make sure you're still awake.

Novelties are great, but sometimes it's best to stick to the more conventional way of doing things. Learn about the standard viewpoints in **IDEAS 21, 22 and 24.**

Try another idea...

If you're writing in a first-person viewpoint, especially one confessional in tone, this seems perfectly normal – just look at D. B. C. Pierre's *Vernon God Little.* If you're writing with a third-person narrator, however, addressing your readers explicitly may direct their attention away from the events of the text and towards its construction. All of a sudden, this disembodied, neutral observer has developed an opinion, and is talking to you like you're its best friend.

If you want an example of how second-person narration is used to excellent effect, read Italo Calvino's *If On a Winter's Night a Traveller.* Here, the narrator begins the tale by instructing you, the reader, to lie down, relax with the book, and tell your friends not to interrupt your reading – almost like an instruction manual for enjoying the book. It alerts you to the novel's artifice, but it also creates a welcome sense of intimacy between the narrator and the reader.

'YOU decide which route to take, which creatures to fight and which dangers to risk! Part story, part game, this is a book with a difference, one in which YOU become the hero!'
STEVE JACKSON and IAN LIVINGSTONE, Fighting Fantasy authors

Defining idea...

How did it go?

Q **I'm dying to use the second person but don't fancy writing an entire story or poem in that style. Can I switch between the second person and another narrative style in a piece of prose or poetry?**

A *Some writers switch between a third-person narrative and a second person to enhance a heightened emotion, showing a character's interior monologue: 'He looked at her, fingering the cold ring in his pocket. You have to do this, it's all up to you now. If you don't propose, she'll never come back. Trying not to panic, he lowered himself on to one knee.' In a context like this, the switch doesn't seem out of place because it reflects his interior monologue – it's the character talking to himself, not to you – but used too often, or used in a situation that doesn't require it, and it will look rather odd.*

Q **I've tried the exercise above, but it's sounding just like a self-help book! How can I make my second-person narration more personal?**

A *It's tricky to get your head round the idea that second-person narration doesn't have to be synonymous with bossiness. You're not trying to tell the reader what to do, you're not even trying to give them suggestions. What you are doing is transferring them directly into the mind of a character; making them, for the duration of the narrative, complicit with events on the page. The key is to try and write as you would with any other narrative style – engaging with the characters and their emotional experience. Don't be fooled into thinking you have to write differently, that you have to give directions in a self-help manner or distance yourself from a character, just because of the unusual narrative style.*

24

Through the eyes of the beholder

If you're looking for an intense and surprising narrative viewpoint, try the first person. Anybody or anything you like can be telling the story – the trick is to avoid 'I' becoming 'you'.

The first-person viewpoint is all about the 'I', the character's sight, their frame of mind, their limited understanding of themselves and the world around them.

With the first person, everything is seen through a single 'I'. Think of the difference in effect between 'he thrusts in the knife, feeling her skin rip' and 'I thrust in the knife, feeling her skin rip.' The 'I' narrator speaks from a privileged position: he or she (or even it) inhabits the world of your text, and is part and parcel of what goes on within. Events therefore have more power to spill off the page and into the reader's consciousness.

Here's an idea for you...

Pick a scenario where you meet your character-narrator and write about it from your own point of view. Then rewrite it from the point of view of your character (write both sketches in the first person). The sketch should include dialogue and interior monologue – explain how you feel, what you want from the situation, your emotional state and so on. This will help you identify the similarities and differences between you and your character, and whether they need to be worked on.

SEEING IS BELIEVING

But there are some restrictions to this point of view. How do you describe your character without risking cliché by having her look in a mirror? Also, everything in the text has to be something known by the narrator, and told through her unique narrative style. She can't see what's coming, she can't see what's happening in another room, she can't tell what other people are thinking, and she doesn't know the truth about everything that has happened (four excellent reasons why this viewpoint is often used in detective fiction).

Moreover, first-person narrators aren't always reliable: how often have you embellished a story to boost somebody's opinion of you? First-person narrators telling somebody else's story (think *Heart of Darkness*) are at even more of a disadvantage. Work out before you start writing exactly what your narrator knows, and how much of what she says should be considered the truth.

SPEAKING FROM THE HEART

We all tell stories from a first-person viewpoint – how many times do you use the word 'I' in a sentence? Because of this, it's easy to see the first person as the most immediate and accessible form in which to write. This way, all of your experiences and knowledge can be drawn upon on demand, and little is lost in the translation to a third person. The first-person narrator also inspires a kind of intimacy that is absent from the more detached third-person alternative. The narrator is speaking from the heart, confessing to you, sharing an experience.

Learn more about investigating a character's past in IDEA 18, *There may be trouble ahead.*

Try another idea...

BEWARE THE CLONE ARMY

But this complicity between the author and the narrator can often be the downfall of both. Because the 'I' is so familiar, the character using it can quickly lose her own identity and become merged with yours. Instead of forming rounded, autonomous characters, you risk simply creating extensions of yourself, each with the same form of speech, the same opinions, the same personality. If your characters are missing the spark that makes them appear unique – if a reader can tell that you're blatantly speaking through them – then nobody is going to be interested in their progress for more than a few pages.

Keeping your characters alive and independent in the first person can be extremely difficult. The trick to succeeding is to ensure that you know each player intimately – their pasts, their dreams, their fears, their pet hates, their political opinions, everything about them – so that they don't risk becoming literary versions of yourself. They are as much a separate construct as a third-person character. The weaker the character appears in your own head, the less chance he has of staying afloat in the seething mass of ideas and images that is your text.

'Give a man a mask and he will reveal himself.'
OSCAR WILDE

Defining idea...

How did it go?

Q **I'm experimenting with first-person narrators and have found myself using animals and even inanimate objects to tell my story. Is it time to call the men in white coats?**

A *Of course not. One of the great benefits of writing from the first person is that your narrator can be anything you like. I've read stories and poems narrated by teddy bears, beetles, buckets, corpses and even weirder things. Novelty narrators such as these can be fun and revealing in short pieces of writing, but think twice about using them for a novel – they can be extremely restrictive, and may end up boring your readers.*

Q **I'm trying this idea's exercise but the character I'm using is completely different to me. How can I make her seem realistic?**

A *Paradoxically, you stand more chance of creating a realistic character if it is nothing like yourself. Look at Mark Twain and Huckleberry Finn. Just make sure you know your character inside out before you start writing – try and live things the way they would.*

Q **So how do I get a character to describe herself without looking in the mirror?**

A *Having a character look in the mirror near the beginning of a story just so the reader gets a visual impression of them is cheesy (although still used all the time). Instead, try getting the character to think of herself: let her find a photo of herself when she was a child and compare it to how she looks now, or have her meet someone and let her think self-consciously or proudly about her appearance.*

25

Too many cooks

A piece of fiction can come to resemble the Black Hole of Calcutta – sweaty, noisy and horrible to be in. Learn to avoid this by restraining your cast.

One of the great questions a writer faces is deciding how many main characters to use in a text, and who gets to hold the reins.

Often, the storyline follows one, perhaps two, protagonists, but if you're not careful, everybody will start shouting for their right to free speech and all you have left is a noisy mess. Be clear from the start whose story you're writing, and make sure you hand out gags to everybody else.

SPOILING THE BROTH

If you're writing in the first person, it's easier to keep control. Generally speaking, the reader is privy to a single character, and sees everybody else through that character's eyes. But this doesn't mean you can't bend the rules a little. If you want to give equal priority to two or more characters, try making the first-person narrator a more neutral observer – look at Nick in *The Great Gatsby*, for example. This way, although the narrator is telling the story, his attention – and the reader's – is shared between several characters.

Here's an idea for you...

Write a scene with multiple characters. How about a controversial boardroom meeting or a family gathering where the daughter blurts out she's pregnant? Start by making brief outlines of everybody there, then decide what kind of viewpoint you want to adopt. It's up to you whether you stick with the one viewpoint or try and fit everybody in. Experiment with the suggestions above until you've found a style you're comfortable with, and one that's not too confusing for a reader.

Of course, you can also use more than one first-person narrator in a piece of writing, but it isn't easy. Readers get used to being in somebody's head, and if they are suddenly wrenched into the mind of another character it can feel disruptive, potentially ruining the experience of reading. There are ways around this, however. You could use chapters to separate the first-person viewpoints, making it obvious (by titles, or by speech and narrative style) whose chapter it is – read Graham Swift's *Last Orders.* Or try dividing the novel into parts, each with a different narrator telling the same story. John Fowles did this to excellent effect in *The Collector.*

THE THIRD MAN

Likewise, using dual or multiple characters in a third-person narrative can pose a few problems. If you've got two or more main characters, who do you follow when they are apart? Making sure you tag along with the right character can seem tricky, but it's easy to get the hang of it. If you ask horror or thriller writers how they keep track of multiple protagonists, they'll tell you the secret is in ensuring they have a common cause, a shared source of conflict.

DON'T ALL TALK AT ONCE

Another complication authors face when writing with several main characters is deciding who gets priority when they all meet up. If there is more than one character in a situation, then it can be tempting to switch back and forth between their thoughts faster than a pinball at full pelt. Check out the example below.

If you're using more than one main character, look at IDEA 27, *Changing lanes*, for some ideas on switching between viewpoints.

Try another idea...

WILMA AND BILLY

'Wilma trotted up to the school gates. Billy hadn't seen her yet, he was talking to a cluster of his tiny friends. She was so proud of him, and she'd show him that now. Bending over, she planted a giant kiss on his cheek.

"Mum!" he hissed, squirming. He hated when she embarrassed him in front of his friends like this.

Wilma straightened herself, pretending not to notice her son's dismissal. Why were the other kids sniggering? What was wrong with a little motherly affection?'

Readers forced to jump in and out of various characters will soon grow tired. Develop a strong narrative voice by picking one character to focus on. A single viewpoint provides a smoother ride:

'We are stupider at some times than others; we can enter into people's minds occasionally but not always, because our own minds get tired; and this intermittence lends in the long run variety and colour to the experiences we receive.'
E. M. FORSTER

Defining idea...

'Billy saw his mum approaching out of the corner of his eye. Great, he thought, she'd want to show him how proud she was, how much she loved him. And right here in front of Davey and his crew. He turned his head in the hope she'd miss him, but she homed in and planted the sloppiest kiss on his cheek.

"Mum!" he hissed, squirming. He could see Davey sniggering, and he knew he'd hurt her feelings. Now she'd be funny with him all afternoon.'

How did it go?

Q **I'm using multiple main characters, but it's getting out of hand. They seem to be revolting against me and taking over the castle! Any hints?**

A *If you've bitten off a little more than you can chew with the number of main characters fighting to tell the story, don't worry. Pick some of the weaker characters and reduce their story to a subplot – seen through the eyes of the characters you let remain central.*

Q **I'm trying the boardroom scene and it's all getting very heated. Are there any other ways of indicating the viewpoints of central characters without explicitly showing what they're thinking?**

A *One easy way of having fewer central characters, but keeping the appearance of more, is to use virtual shifts. Instead of shifting from one character's point of view to another's, use subtly placed adverbs to hint at what another character is thinking or feeling. There are a million and one adverbs available for use – obviously, clearly, ostensibly, presumably – each of which influences the way the reader interprets the action. Instead of writing from Wilma's point of view, try an adverb: 'Billy watched his mother, clearly upset and angry at his behaviour, storm back to the car.' Too many of these, though, can make your writing look clumsy.*

26

It's all in the past

Or is it? Here's how to select the right tense for your fiction, and some ideas to help you decide whether or not to obey the rules.

At first glance, we're all rooted in the 'now'. I am writing this idea in my office, sitting on a comfy chair that my cat is currently trying to chew to bits. Shoo.

TIME BANDITS

You probably haven't given a great deal of thought to what tense you'll be writing in. It's considered common practice to regale stories in the past tense and to write screenplays in the present. Poetry has always been a law unto itself, but the poets among you may find you stick to a particular tense when writing, and that anything else feels slightly strange. Practically our entire experience of literature railroads us down certain temporal tracks when writing – fairy tales, newspapers, schoolbooks and most novels all talk about events in the past tense. But these tracks are guidelines, not rules. You can, if you want, time travel.

Here's an idea for you...

Take something you've written in the past tense (alternatively use another author's text). Now rewrite it in the present tense. You'll probably miss a few verbs, but don't worry. When you've finished, look back at the piece and compare how each version makes you feel. Is the rewritten piece harder to read, or more difficult to believe? Or does it present events in a much more intimate way than the original?

LOOKING BACK

If you think about it, writing in the past tense makes a fair bit of sense. You can't, after all, recount events until after they've happened (unless, of course, you're recounting them to yourself or to somebody with you at the time). Because of this, the past tense can retain more credibility than the present – it can seem a little odd to have a narrator divulging their story as it unfolds: shouldn't they be focusing on events in hand?

TENSING UP

But even within the past tense there is a little freedom. Now brace yourself for grammar lesson flashbacks – you'll probably be writing in the simple past tense (which posh folk call the preterit), as in 'he sat down on the stained leather seat'. When writing in the past tense it's always best to stick to the simple past – this is the present of your story, the moment events are occurring in your characters' eyes. But if you want to delve even further into the past, you've got the option of the past perfect (pluperfect), as in 'he had sat on that filthy seat for hours before the nurse agreed to see him'.

You can also bear in mind the past progressive, which is used to describe events that began in the past but are continuing in the story's present: 'he was sitting on the chair feeling miserable when the nurse walked in'; and the past perfect progressive, which denotes events that began in the past and ended in the past: 'he had been sitting on the chair when the nurse walked in'. Including the odd mixed tense can help keep a text fresh and can provide great opportunities for character flashbacks and exposition.

See IDEAS 35 and 36 for other tips on handling the passage of time in your work.

Try another idea...

BACK TO THE FUTURE

Some creative writers consider it a cardinal sin to mix the past and the present. It is, but only if you do it carelessly. One trick for juggling your tenses is to mix action in the past tense with a present tense interior monologue. Instead of 'He arched his back, trying to get comfortable. Two hours now, he thought, scowling at the empty reception desk, how much longer would he have to wait?' try 'He arched his back, trying to get comfortable. I'm not waiting much longer, if she doesn't come out of that door in ten minutes I'm gone.' This mix can provide a bridge between a storyteller's narrative tone and the more intimate present first person.

CHRISTMAS PRESENTS

Entire narratives written in the present tense appear much less frequently than their historical cousins. Saying that, the technique is becoming more and more common, with many writers using the tense experimentally in order to forge a more intimate relationship between the main character and the reader. And it can be extremely effective. 'I strike him on the

Marty McFly; 'Are you telling me you built a time machine into a DeLorean?'
Doc Emmett Brown: 'The way I see it, if you're gonna build a time machine into a car, why not do it with some style?'
Back to the Future

Defining idea...

115

nose, feeling bone shatter and sinew twist' leaps out in a more immediate, startling way than 'I struck him on the nose, feeling bone shatter and sinew twist'. If readers get past the strange illusion of watching events as they unfold, the experience of reading a present tense narrative can be exhilarating.

How did it go?

Q   **I'm rewriting a text in the present but it's a little repetitive. Are there different forms of present tense I can use to break things up?**

A   *You mean you're not sick of the grammar already? Yes, there are various forms of present tense you can use. It's best to stick to the simple present: 'he sits there'. You can also use the present perfect: 'he has sat there all day', the present progressive: 'he is sitting there' and the present perfect progressive (I've never seen so many Ps on a single page): 'he has been sitting there all day'. These last three can be added in periodically when writing prose, and can be used in poetry to create various different atmospheres.*

Q   **While we're on the subject of time travel, what are the rules for using flashbacks in fiction?**

A   *There are no set rules. The only real difficulties are knowing when to insert a flashback and how to let readers know they're going back in time. Don't take the easy way out and write the date of the flashback – readers will know what's happening with a few subtle clues in the first few lines. And make sure a flashback is justified: too much time travel, or time travel without a clear purpose, will just end up confusing. One alternative to a full-on flashback is to have a character think back to his past: 'He remembered how he'd met her...'*

27

Changing lanes

Your narrative style should steer readers – although we're talking a gentle hand on the arm, not a guide dog. Sometimes, though, it can be exciting to let go and give the reader a real wake-up call.

It's always tempting to play around with viewpoint and tense in your writing.

Feel free to experiment when you're exercising and plotting, it can be a great way to get to know your own writing style. But resist the temptation to become a dark lord of time and space when writing a finished piece. Like some evil Doctor Who villain you may upset more than just your characters by jumbling up your points of view and darting back and forth between time zones.

ANARCHY!

You can use viewpoint and tense any way you like in your fiction – there are no fixed codes of practice. Go nuts, try a literary pick 'n' mix. Many novelists and short story writers have played with unusual ideas and come up trumps, hailed as the pioneers of new narrative styles. Many more have also tried, but emerged with horribly mutated stories that nobody can understand. Whatever you do, ask yourself if it's justified in terms of the plot. If you're mixing and matching for a reason, great; if you're doing it to look clever, don't.

Here's an idea for you... **Think back to a time when you've been under extreme pressure. Try to recapture what was going through your mind. Now, write a short piece describing the incident, but use a variety of narrative styles to convey the emotional turbulence of the situation. You may start off in the third-person limited, then zoom in to the first person, before retreating to an omniscient point of view. You'll probably never use the end result, but the exercise should help you fine-tune your narrative skills.**

THE INNER VOICE

If you're anything like me, you spend half the day talking to yourself (not always out loud). Take the time to listen to that voice and those interior dialogues, analyse their narrative form. Usually, my inner voice adopts the same narrative style as my real voice – in other words it's a first-person narrator. If I'm stressed, however, or have committed a disastrous *faux pas* in company, it becomes confused, and I quite often find it addressing me as 'he' (imagining myself from another's point of view: 'he really should have finished Idea 27 by now') or 'you' (as in 'you complete plonker, Gordon'). We don't always see ourselves from a straight and simple perspective, and a 'realistic' narrative would reflect this through an oscillating point of view. It just so happens that literary convention favours simplicity, but if you are feeling brave, and you want to reflect a character's turbulent emotional state, try experimenting with a mixed narrative style.

MAKING A STATEMENT

Used cleverly, such abrupt or unexplained changes in narrative style and tense can serve to enhance the theme and feel of a piece of writing. In *The Blood of Others*, Simone de Beauvoir does exactly this. Set during the Second World War, the novel uses a highly experimental structure, mixing various narrative styles in a seemingly random fashion. It should all end up as a confused mess, yet it doesn't. De Beauvoir has toyed with the conventions of narrative, but has left enough for her readers to be able to navigate. It can be hard at times, but you rarely lose sense of where you are or whose head you're in. Instead, the fractured narrative style adds to the powerful sense of confusion and impotence that every character feels, and as a reader you achieve a much more profound sense of empathy. If you want to create a deliberate sense of confusion or claustrophobia, try mixing narrative styles or writing in different tenses. Just listen to your inner voice – if you get confused, you can be sure your reader will too.

Careful plotting will ensure that your creative play doesn't result in confusion: check out IDEA 34, *Every which way but loose*, for some pointers.

Try another idea...

THE SIMPLE LIFE

Whatever the smug literary academic who lives next door says, it's OK to be simple. There's absolutely nothing wrong with using a consistent viewpoint and tense. Look back at the books you've really enjoyed. How many use complicated, shifting narrative techniques? Not many of my favourites do. You're telling a story, and while sometimes you may need to play with the rules in order to make a point (about literature, or about the world), most of the time you just want to keep readers engaged.

'The thing about writers that people don't realize is that a lot of what they do is play.'
MARGARET ATWOOD

Defining idea...

How did it go?

Q   **I've written my piece but I can't really gauge how much sense it makes. It's easy for me to tell what's going on because I wrote it, but how do I know if it'll make sense to anybody else?**

A   *The best thing to do is simply to ask somebody else to read it. Ask them honestly whether they could follow what was going on, or whether the narrative style was too confusing. Even if they did become a little lost, it's not the end of the world – if they felt a sense of confusion, panic, embarrassment or denial when reading, then you know you've been successful. With this exercise, evoking feeling is just as important as narrative flow.*

Q   **I'm trying new changes in viewpoint but I'm finding it hard to keep track. I check back over my work regularly but each time I do I get more and more confused. Is there any way to avoid tying myself in knots?**

A   *According to David Lodge, constantly checking for inconsistencies in your work is one of the most common signs of an inexperienced writer. When writing, trust your instincts and keep writing. Don't keep going back to check for errors, as you'll end up tying yourself in knots. Read back after every chapter or verse, not after every line, and you'll have a much better sense of where your work is heading.*

28

Virtual realty

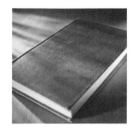

So, you've recruited your characters, you know them intimately and even have an inkling of where they're heading – but don't get so carried away with the drama that you forget about the setting in which it unfolds.

You can't cast John Gielgud as King Lear, usher him onto a pink plastic stage set and expect people not to snigger.

Your characters – no matter how existential they are – need a world around them (even the characters of *Waiting For Godot* have a tree and a crossroad). Readers expect nothing else. Think of your favourite literary heroes (or villains) and I'll bet their surroundings pop up with them. Marlow on his Congo steamer surrounded by the dark forest; Winston Smith amidst the antique junk of the store as he waits for Julia, or deep in the bowels of the Ministry, in Room 101. Characters need to be tied down in a place and time, given context, if they are to become believable in the eyes of a reader.

PEEPING TOM'S CABIN

We are instinctively nosy creatures; we want to know how other people live, what secrets lie hidden in their cupboard. Fiction lets you look around characters' homes

Here's an idea for you...

Pick a character from your writing that you know relatively well, and place him in your own home. It's the first time he's been there. Write a couple of hundred words from his point of view, concentrating on the things you think he'd pick up on about the way you live. Then 'beam' him to a new location. What's the first thing he notices there? Beam your character to as many new locations as you like, each one stranger and more surreal than the last.

without their knowing. What you see isn't put on for the cameras – smiles, neatness, colour – it's them in their natural habitat, warts and all. You can pry into every nook, peer into every cranny, poke under every floorboard, without anybody ever realising you've been there.

OPTICAL ALLUSIONS

A reader's relationship with your literary world is tentative: not enough reminders of where they are and they will drift back to their own place and time; too many and the effect will be ruined, snapping them back to reality quicker than a slap on the face. The trick is to tread lightly, stay subtle. If you're planning to start off along the lines of 'It was a dark and stormy night in New York', don't leave it there. OK, we all know what New York looks like, but our mental picture is general, imprecise, and boring because of it. We don't know what New York looks like to your character, the details that are important to him, which he notices first.

SIZE DOESN'T MATTER

It's not enough to assume that readers will conjure up the world around your character based on an initial statement. If you don't keep laying on subtle reminders, the mental image they have will soon grow fuzzy and unappealing. Start with the small details, the ones that matter most. Think about the first things you notice when you arrive at a new location: the smell of lavender, the way the ivy clings to the graffiti-strewn walls, the cold air on your cheeks, the sounds of a car engine turning over. You don't necessarily notice the grand picture first off, and your characters probably won't either.

Setting can help reveal the inner depths of your characters – see IDEA 30, *Keeping up with the Joneses.*

Try another idea...

So when setting the scene, start by describing the details that mean something to your characters, the small points they might notice above all else – aim to capture a character's emotional engagement with his surroundings. That way, not only will the scene stay fresh and vibrant in the reader's mind, it will also reveal more about your characters and the way they view the world.

Of course, there's only so much detail a person can take in at any given point. If you're writing in the first person, or the third-person limited, you need to restrain your creative urge when describing a fictional world: unless your character is obsessive, it's doubtful whether they'd notice the fluff under the couch, the number of pennies in the jar or how many glittering pendants are dangling from the chintzy lampshade. Even if you're taking a wider narrative scope, limit how much descriptive information you provide. The aim is to make the setting personal and realistic, not to imitate a scene of crime report. Take D. H. Lawrence's advice and look for the objects that are alive, which resonate with energy, which are special, which are used.

'*The author must know his countryside, whether real or imagined, like his hand.*'
ROBERT LOUIS STEVENSON

Defining idea...

How did it go?

Q **I'm trying the above exercise but I've always told my characters never to go to new places by themselves. Can I use more than one character?**

A *Yes, and it can work even better this way. Pick two or three characters and place them in the same location at the same time. The more complex and individual the characters, the better the result. Each one should pick up on different aspects of their location; each will be fascinated by different details. Working out what and why can really help you develop realistic scenes and characters.*

Q **I'm putting in a lot of detail about my setting, but it still doesn't have a great deal of depth. Where am I going wrong?**

A *Part of the problem with putting in extensive detail is putting in too much. You don't want to try and create an itinerary of objects in a place. Instead you need to pick the details that mean something to the character, and which influence their experience of a location. Another common problem is a lack of definition in a description. Don't just write 'tree', give it its proper name: 'oak' or 'ash'. This will give you a greater appearance of authority, and help more clearly define the scene.*

29

Changing rooms

Everywhere, no matter how mundane, has an atmosphere. Learn to tune into this in order to create a three-dimensional, multi-sensory world.

'Doctor Who' used to scare the pants off me. But all it took to drag me back rudely to the real world was for a rock to wobble as an advancing Dalek sidled into it.

ATMOSPHERIC PRESSURE

You need to bring your setting to life. You have to breathe enough magic into those descriptive words to transport a reader into another world, another place and time. This means not only writing well, but also seeing well. Whatever the location, from something as prosaic as a post office to as sensational as a space shuttle, it has its own presence – a unique atmosphere embodied in its layout, design, history, location and relationship to people. It's vital to pin down the elements of a place that give it this atmosphere if it's to seem genuine on the page.

Honing your powers of description just takes practice and, above all, experience. You should be aiming to make the reader feel as though they've visited somewhere

Here's an idea for you...

Go and visit a favourite location: a park, a cemetery, a shopping mall, a gallery. Settle somewhere out of the way with a cup of coffee and spend some hours observing and making notes. Begin by noting the tiniest of details, then start to build a more complete picture of your surroundings. Try and see it through the eyes of one of your characters – what fascinates/irritates/elevates her most? Before long, you'll have created a cumulative build-up of detail, soaking your reader in the ambience of a location.

personally by the time they've finished reading. This means using all of your skills and all of your resources to create a rich, three-dimensional, multi-sensory setting.

GETTING TO KNOW YOU

Do your research. Just because you've physically been in a place doesn't mean you've looked at it carefully: don't take it for granted. Keep your eyes peeled for the small details, the things that usually remain hidden from view: the way the light hits the buildings, the dog hair on the carpet, the way the computers whirr. Jot a plan down in a notebook, including doodles if you want, so you've got a list of these insights – as well as more mundane descriptions of furniture, objects, décor – to hand. Even if you never use half of it, it gives you a much clearer mental picture of your location.

And remember, just because you can visualise your location when you read back through your work doesn't mean a reader will. You've had the advantage of actually being there (or, if not, having researched and imagined it for hours on end). In order to ensure your reader can picture a scene as clearly as you do, it's vital first to be able to approach it as they will: from outside. Don't risk becoming too familiar with your literary locations, try and see them freshly, without prejudice, as if you'd never encountered them before. Again, this means looking at the small details, the ones even you've never noticed before.

PLAYING AWAY

Of course, you may not be able to visit the scenes you're using in person. If they're historical, they may not exist any more; if they're political, you may not have access; if it's a foreign country you're describing, you may not have enough cash to get there and back; and if you're writing sci-fi- well, you can't very well nip across to Venus for a research trip. But this doesn't mean you get off lightly. Use every resource you can to learn more about the setting. Talk to people who have lived there, watch movies filmed in the same location, look on the internet, read relevant novels, travel guides, holiday reviews, astronomy books and street plans. You need to be able to answer any questions about your setting (even if you're the only one doing the asking).

Even your own home can be an exotic place to write about. Check out IDEA 31, *There's no place like home.*

Try another idea...

ABOVE ALL...

Above all, remember this: when setting the scene in your work you need to be able to recreate it, not just set out a list of details. Before you can do this, you need to be able to exist in that scene in your mind, to be able to see, hear, smell, touch and taste as if you are actually there. Only by supplying these sensory details will you be able to carry the reader with you. Look at John Steinbeck's *Of Mice and Men* – the first paragraph in every chapter is a master class in creating powerful description.

'Everybody has to be somewhere.'
SPIKE MILLIGAN

Defining idea...

How did
it go?

Q **I've tried sitting in a location writing down details, but I can't concentrate on what I'll need for the finished piece of writing, and always end up with too much. How can I be more selective?**

A   *When you're sitting observing like this, don't concern yourself with the finished product. The idea is to pinpoint what it is about a place that makes it special, so just jot down any impressions you get. It's too much to try and form your notes into a complete setting there and then. Wait until you're back at home, then you can look back through the notes and pick out the most evocative descriptions.*

Q **Visiting a place is fine if it's the park across the street or the local volleyball courts, but what if I want to write about somewhere I don't like?**

A   *Well, bite the bullet and visit it, notebook at the ready. If you really don't feel comfortable in a place, great. Sit down and try and figure out why. Make notes in the same fashion – from the ground up – until you have built up a bigger picture. You'll be able to present a much more convincing portrait of a location this way. Of course, if the place is Death Alley it might be best to rely on other resources and your own imagination – just be careful.*

30

Keeping up with the Joneses

A person's surroundings are more than just wrapping paper. The places people go and the objects they interact with can reveal more about them than they like to think – use this hidden language for powerful characterisation.

Have you ever wondered why your elderly neighbour keeps the black, withered remains of dried roses on her windowsill? Or why your mate's parents fill their dusty, quiet house with lurid, heart-shaped valentine pillows?

Where a person lives, and the objects they choose to surround themselves with, can say a great deal about them. Taking care over your literary sets can allow you to reveal your characters much more subtly and efficiently than most other more direct mechanisms. So be careful when you're moving that vase...

WHAT DOES YOUR LOO SAY ABOUT YOU?

You may have seen the advert for toilet cleaner, with the slogan 'What does your loo say about you?' Quite a bit, I should think, and not just your loo, either. There's

Here's an idea for you... **Create a room from scratch and then ask others to guess who inhabits it. The room can be anywhere, in any time. Start your description from a focal point. Try and use the room's contents to give clues about who lives there. Don't be too clichéd or vague, and provide everything relevant with depth. And don't just catalogue items: pick the objects dear to your anonymous character. When you're finished, pass it around and see how accurately your fellow writers or friends can picture the room and its owner.**

a saying that if you strip a person of their surroundings, their belongings, their house then they're no longer that person. That's a tad extreme (reality TV 'stars' always seem to remain their irritating selves), but there's a lot to be said for how much your surroundings say about you. People immerse themselves in a world that makes them feel comfortable, they decorate for a reason, they line the walls with possessions because they mean something to them. You can use this powerful sense of association to great effect in your writing.

OBJECTS WITH VOICES

Returning to my opening example, which of the following would attract more empathy in a piece of fiction? 'The lonely old lady stared absently out of the window. I miss him so much, she thought, thinking of her beloved Alfie. Why did he have to die after remaining her husband for 48 years?' or 'The old lady stared absently out the window, fingering the desiccated roses. Alfie had bought them her, the last thing he'd done. She'd never forget the gesture, she thought, even as another black petal crumbled to dust beneath her touch.'

OK, neither is going to reduce you to tears, but the cringe-worthy piece of self-pity expressed through internal monologue in the first quote can easily be replaced by a subtle action in the second. The crumbling roses are a little clichéd in this example, but it shows how an object can be metaphorical (here demonstrating the fragility of the old woman's memory) as well as merely physical. You can still use other mechanisms to express how a character is feeling, but by showing them interacting with their environment – especially a place personal to them – you can present a much more vivid and convincing picture of their state of mind.

Look more closely at metaphors and other forms of symbolism in IDEAS 5 and 12.

Try another idea...

THAT'S PATHETIC

My English teacher used to go on about 'pathetic fallacy' all the time – how the things that surround a character provide an insight into their state of mind, how what was on the outside could mirror what lay within. I could never really understand why the technique had such a bizarre name, but I guess that's beside the point. The attribution of human characteristics to the outside world has been used for centuries to enhance the mood of a piece of writing and to allow characters to reveal their true thoughts without the need to speak or think.

For a good example, just think of practically any horror book or film: how often is the fear of a protagonist expressed by the violent thunderstorm above? Or, just so my English teacher doesn't think I've forgotten, think of *Wuthering Heights*, and the way the moors reflects Cathy's stormy emotional state. As with everything, however, don't get silly (unless it's intentional, of course). Your character's frame of mind may occasionally be reflected in their surroundings, but if it happens all the time then something is very wrong.

'We write to taste life twice.'
ANAÏS NIN

Defining idea...

How did
it go?

Q **I see what you're saying about objects reflecting emotions. Should I start making everything in my writing symbolic?**

A *Only make objects metaphorical if you think it reveals more about a character or their frame of mind. Objects and surroundings don't have to be metaphorical to make a statement about their owner. People adjust their personalities depending on where they are. Think about how much you change when you're in a meeting, out on the town, visiting your partner's parents. By exploring how your character reacts to different scenes, you can present a more rounded personality to the reader.*

Q **I'm finding it hard to reveal information about my characters through the setting. Are there any other tricks?**

A *Of course. Don't just rely on your setting to develop or reveal your characters, use your descriptive powers to take a closer look at your characters, to zoom in, as it were, on their own expressive landscape. This works especially well in emotional scenes. Investigate your characters' actions and reactions with a magnifying glass – note the beads of sweat forming on the forehead, the lip twitching, the fingers trembling.*

Q **I'm on a tight schedule. Do I have to look for the detail in every scene?**

A *You should try to. Even if you're just scene-setting, try to evoke as much drama and feeling into the setting as possible. This way, readers won't get bored in the bits between the main action.*

31

There's no place like home

Look around you at the place you live, really look around. Familiarity may have made it seem a little dull, but this is your world, and it's too valuable a resource to ignore.

OK, so you don't live on Mars, or even some idyllic tropical isle. But hold up. Before you launch into a piece of writing set half a world or more away, take another look around you.

The literary grass may seem greener in Hong Kong or Mexico City, but believe me, no place is richer in your mind than your home town. I'm not saying become a local writer (god forbid). But we are all intimately linked with the landscape in which we live. So make the most of it!

THIS IS A LOCAL SHOP, FOR LOCAL PEOPLE

Few things send a shiver down a writer's spine like the words 'local writer'. We all want to encompass the grander things in our work, the universal truths of humankind, and we're adamant that there's no chance of finding that in the village shop. It's odd that a great many of us feel that other locations are somehow richer, stranger, more exciting than our own backyards. It's an illusion brought about by

Here's an idea for you...

Walk through your home and try and describe it as a stranger would. Record the smallest details – remember: you've got five senses. Now learn to play with what you see. Fill your notebooks with sketches, doodles, descriptions, and mix reality with fantasy. Imagine who lived there before you, who may move in after you've gone, or in a hundred year's time.

familiarity: any life can seem the paradigm of ordinariness to the person who lives it, and any location you spend a great deal of time in can seem uneventful and plain.

HOME ALONE

I've been editing *The Egg Box* magazine for years now. When it was first founded, I trained myself to look for the most unusual stories and poems: those set in far-flung locations, full of mystery, suspense and intricate, surreal detail. But it didn't work out that way. The writing that really gripped me, the poems and short stories that seemed most unusual, most adventurous, most atmospheric, were the ones set at home. In most cases, the writers who had tried to play away had created hazy, shadowy worlds, lacking in detail and devoid of presence. In short, it was obvious they'd never been there, even to a reader who'd never been there either.

The writers who wrote about home, however (Aberdeen, Sydney, Manchester, Kuala Lumpur, Norwich, San Andreas), knew their world so intimately that they could literally do anything they wanted with it. Most of what they'd written was imaginary, but the world they'd created in which to stage their fictitious action had been painted in such detail it was impossible not to become involved. Likewise, the fact that their history was so obviously entwined with their landscape meant that they could tap into a vast store of emotional energy, consciously or not.

FEELING AT HOME

If you're like most people, then a vast majority of your past experiences and turbulent emotions have occurred at home – your childhood home, your halls of residence, your current house, perhaps a home behind bars. We may spend much of our time imagining we are elsewhere, but we are a product of our surroundings, and have shared so much with them. If only walls could talk. Because of this intimate connection between landscape and emotional experience, looking to your home for inspiration makes more sense than it sounds. It's true what they say: that the universal is embodied in the local, and if you can harness it, it can make your writing extraordinary.

My English teacher would be delighted: writing about home is one way of writing about 'what you know'. See IDEA 6, *Blowing your trumpet*, for a few more.

Try another idea…

OPEN YOUR EYES

As a writer, you have to become a stranger everywhere you go, even if it's a room you've known for decades (in fact, especially if it's a room you've known for decades). Get rid of your assumptions: next time you enter a room you think you know well imagine it's the first time you've visited it, look at everything with a newcomer's curiosity. You'll be amazed to see how much your brain has blanked out, how much it simply takes for granted.

Learn to see past this temporary blindness, look at your home or your home town in detail and allow the memories to come flooding back, and the emotional ammunition with them.

'The man who writes about himself and his own time is the only man who writes about all people and about all time.'
GEORGE BERNARD SHAW

Defining idea…

How did it go?

Q **I'm trying to write about my street but it's turning out like an autobiography, and I'm sure my neighbours won't want to read about their own bizarre habits next time they're browsing in Waterstone's. How can I make it more like fiction?**

A *It's the atmosphere of a place you're trying to capture – you don't necessarily have to include your real neighbours, or even yourself. Blend the physical, sensory presence of your street with dreams and fantasy; let your imagination run wild. Let strangers inhabit the houses, or switch real people around and pair them off in odd ways. Remember, you're the boss; you can set out your street as and how you like. Go on, have some fun.*

Q **So what's wrong with being a local writer then?**

A *According to some people, everything! Just look at what Flannery O'Connor had to say: 'The woods are full of regional writers, and it is the great horror of every serious writer that he will become one of them.' In truth, though, there's absolutely nothing wrong with being a local writer so long as you still try and embody the grander themes in your work, the important questions about the human condition. In other words, as long as you put as much passion and creativity in your work as you would writing about any less parochial subject. If you find yourself writing a novel on your village hall, then maybe it's time to heed O'Connor's words...*

32

Poetic licence

Novels, stories and screenplays aren't the only things that need a setting. Poetry also relies on the visual to convey a sense of mood and meaning. But when writing a poem, a great deal more depends on how you choose to decorate.

Setting the scene in a poem can be a tricky bugger to get right.

Finding the right mix of appropriate and illuminating detail, without swamping a poem with surplus, extravagant description, is like trying to balance a human pyramid on your shoulders: one slip and it can all topple into an obscure and meaningless jumble of parts. When setting the scene, stay sharp, and think hard about why you're including certain elements of a place and discarding others. Only this scrupulous selection of detail can keep a good poem from turning fuzzy.

MOOD SETTERS

When writing, don't be tempted to include every single detail you pick up on. If you've been working on a poem for a while, you've probably thought about it a great deal, mulling things over in your mind, working on new ways to describe the scene, the events, the characters. It's easy to build up a vast storehouse of descriptive phrases and symbolic meanings, most of which you're quite chuffed with. But when it comes to piecing it together into a poem, you need to get out

Here's an idea for you...

Make a short list of items that interest you. Pick the object that fascinates you most, and jot down thoughts, phrases, memories and associations. Forget the poem: simply let your imagination loose. Compare the object with everything you can think of and make a note of the most surprising metaphors – be as daring or ridiculous as you like. With luck, these associations and metaphors will start to solidify into a poem.

your fluff filter. It's unlikely that everything you've thought of can go in, even if you're writing an epic, so it's up to you to pick the parts that do the most work.

It's important to try and build up detail in an efficient and effective way. OK, that sounds more like a statement from *52 Brilliant Ideas for Your Business Plan* than a writing guide but don't ignore it because of fears it may impede your creative urge. With poetry, it's not so much about setting a visual scene as setting an atmospheric one. Of course you want to paint a picture, but aim to use your images sparsely, allowing them to accumulate, to build on one another until they create or embody the mood of the whole poem. Even if your single images don't say a great deal in themselves, if you control them, they'll work cumulatively, complementing one another to create a whole much greater than the sum of its parts.

USE THE FORCE

Another similar setback to writing powerful poetry is a lack of clarity. If it's in the right place, then a descriptive image doesn't have to be long and complex to pack a punch. Don't dress your images up with clumsy adjectives purely for the sake of appearances. A wrong choice may distance the reader from the image, forcing them to think too hard about what you're trying to say – what exactly are the *contemplative* leaves? Even a more pertinent image could steer a reader's interpretation too firmly, railroading them into a particular understanding: 'her unkind gaze'. It's hard to stay subtle, but remember that in most cases, when placed well, a concrete image is sufficient on its own.

Learn more about using metaphors wonderfully not wastefully in IDEA 5, *Shall I compare thee to a summer's day?*

Try another idea…

SPEAKING METAPHORICALLY

Used with caution, metaphorical images – those that hint at something more than the image itself – can add a great deal to a poem, turning it from a literal description into a powerfully symbolic and personal piece of writing. But beware – metaphors used too often have another name, clichés, and it's best to stay well clear of anything you recognise from everyday usage. Instead, invent your own metaphors. Pick objects that you associate with emotions and experience and ask yourself why? What is it about an inanimate object that brings to mind an ethereal, emotional equivalent? When writing, you should find metaphors popping up almost naturally – your own mind's way of helping you comprehend the subject of a poem. Use your instinct, and pick the ones that really make you think, the ones so poignant and evocative that they literally make your heart pound.

'*Within the compass of one short poem, dealing with one concrete experience, large questions about love, life and death can be raised.*'
JOHN PECK, US poet

Defining idea…

143

How did it go?

Q **Can I be a little more ambitious with my metaphorical experimentation or should I stick to single metaphors when writing?**

A   *If you're trying to tackle a universal subject, especially one that's difficult or taboo, then you can underpin the entire construction with symbolic meaning – a single metaphor that serves as the foundation for the whole poem. Disguising the heart of the poem with a series of tight, focused images can create a much more intimate, thought-provoking and immediate relationship between the subject and the reader than a more literal text.*

Q **When I'm thinking of metaphors they tend to be either 'light' or 'dark'. Is there such as thing as light and dark imagery or am I being simple?**

A   *According to some critics, just about any poem ever written uses light and dark imagery, with (rather obviously) light reflecting the positive, and dark reflecting the negative tones. These images don't have to be blatant, however, and there's no rule to say you can't reverse them.*

Q **Do I have to give names to the objects I use in poems, or can I leave more to the reader's imagination?**

A   *By all means keep things anonymous – it's a great technique for disturbing a reader. If somebody can't quite put a finger on where the poem is set, or what certain objects or people within it are, it can be very unsettling. You have to compensate for the lack of explicit naming with a clever use of descriptive language, though, or a reader will get completely lost.*

33

Westerns, waterworlds and beavers

It's vital that you pin down the theme of whatever you're writing. Why? Because the theme is the heart of a piece of writing, it's the very blood that flows through it.

People will always ask of a piece of writing 'so what's it about then?' Your first answer will probably be a vague plot description.

They'll then ask 'So what's it really about then?' This time, your answer will most likely be the theme. Theme is the essential idea that runs through your story, its soul. No matter how well you write, a story without a theme is like a tin man without a heart – and it'll take more than a trip to the wizard to fix.

IN FOCUS

Theme parks are so called for a good reason: everything there revolves around one particular idea: the Western, or the Waterworld, or, if it's the crap one near me, Beavers. Leo Tolstoy claimed that every work of art should have a focus, 'some place where all the rays meet or from which they issue'. This focus is the theme, the ideas about the human condition around which the entire fabric of the story revolves. It's the essence of what you want to say.

Here's an idea for you...

If you think you know the theme of something you're currently working on, write it down now. If you've written a convoluted page of waffle, you're either trying to say too much or are not clear about what theme you're trying to embody. If you can pin down your theme in a handful of words, you'll be able to bring your entire screenplay, novel or poem into focus.

WRITING FROM THE HEART

When considering your theme, you only have to remember one thing: it's about being true to yourself, and writing from the heart. Yes, that makes me sound like a hippy, but if you don't delve deep into your own core beliefs and emotions, if you don't discover what themes are important to your own life, you will have nothing of any interest to say in your writing. Look hard at how you see the world; think about what you want to tell people, and what comments you want to make about life.

Even if you're writing a plot-based story of a terrorist attack on Great Yarmouth, the theme that makes the plot work must engage you. Don't be tempted to ignore the theme that's important to you and replace it with one that's hackneyed or clichéd – you'll end up penning a soulless holiday book that's forgotten as soon as it's been put down. Writing must come from the heart as well as the head.

TAKE YOUR TIME

It doesn't matter if you're not sure of your theme when you start a new piece. Some writers set off with a theme in mind, or know what the core of their work will be as soon as they think of their main character; other writers make it three-quarters of the way through their novel, or screenplay, before they pin down exactly what their theme will be. Either way is OK, but what's vital is that eventually you do decide (or let your writing decide for itself) what the theme will be. And remember, theme isn't inherent in a story, but originates from the way a story is told, the way that you as a writer feel about it – the theme underlying 'boy meets girl, girl is killed, boy gets revenge' could be one of romance, anger or guilt depending on your own beliefs.

Themes often pop up hand in hand with an idea, so keep a look out for them when you're reading IDEA 2, *Taking the plunge.*

Try another idea...

HOLDING IT TOGETHER

Whatever theme you decide upon in the end, it will be the core that runs the length of your work, the thread that links events on the page. It's not your job to state your theme explicitly. If you make the point of saying, in the first page, that the story is about the fact that initial impressions aren't necessarily true, or that power corrupts, you spoil the readers' fun – they've got nothing to pull them through, no suspense to entice them.

Instead, think of theme as part and parcel of the development and transformation of your main character. The theme of a piece of writing will be embodied in her actions, in her beliefs, in her world view – another reason why you need to know your characters like you know your own family before you start to write. The theme that develops from your characters will form a thread through the entire piece, a unifying idea that will continuously resurface as your character changes, like a mirror showing their development.

'For a creative writer possession of the "truth" is less important than emotional sincerity.'
GEORGE ORWELL

Defining idea...

147

How did
it go?

Q **I've decided on my theme, and managed to summarise it, but I want to make sure a reader will know what I'm talking about straight away. Will my theme be immediately apparent to a reader?**

A *Not at all. According to Roland Barthes, once a text has been released into the public domain its theme and its meaning becomes protean, mutable, subject to the interpretation of anyone who reads it. In this light, a text can have a million different themes depending on who is reading it. This doesn't mean you should ignore the theme – the more you pull it into focus, the more powerful your work will be, and the more likely it is a reader will be drawn in.*

Q **I'm keen on using a common plot, but am worried about my theme becoming predictably cheesy as a result. Is there any way of avoiding the Camembert effect?**

A *Some folk say that all stories can be categorised into one of a few themes. Don't despair: there is an infinite number of ways to present a theme through fiction. The way you develop your plot and evolve your theme depends on your personality – if you're true to yourself, you'll create a work that resonates in a unique and fascinating way. Think of the way newspaper stories sound completely different depending on the bias of the journalist.*

34

Every which way but loose

You've created your characters. Now it's time for them to do something. Get to grips with plot – the sequence of related events that's the most interesting and dramatically effective way of telling the story.

Fiction without a plot closely resembles a car without wheels. Ignore it and your characters aren't going anywhere — and neither are your readers.

One of the difficulties when considering plot is trying to work out exactly what 'plot' is. It's more than just the story you're working with. E. M. Forster puts it better than I ever could: '"The king died and then the queen died", is a story. "The king died and then the queen died of grief", is a plot. The time sequence is preserved, but the sense of causality overshadows it.' You don't just want a list of events and happenings, you need to include the links between them, the causal chain of events, decisions, responses and repercussions. A good plot is like a chain – only as strong as its weakest link. Without the connections and interactions, it's just a hunk of junk.

Here's an idea for you...

When plotting, draw diagrams on your walls, pin up photographs, make charts, draw maps. These visual aids can help you keep track of an entire plot, no matter how complex, showing you how characters and their relationships are developing. Use these charts to show what emotional state your characters are in, what they've achieved, how they look on life. This way you can keep a track on how believably your characters are developing.

NO COPYING AT THE BACK!

You can't really appreciate the unique qualities of a specific plot until you become aware of how alike novels are in terms of the basic stories and structures they use. It may not seem like it at first glance, but almost all novels use the classical narrative structure: employing a beginning, a middle and an end. In Forster's terms again: 'The queen died, no-one knew why, until it was discovered it was through grief at the death of the king.' Beginning (death), middle (investigation), and end (revelation). Unlike the story, which simply ends without taking the time to answer all the niggling questions, the plot gives an explanation, fills in the links, makes it complete and, more importantly, unique. The story you're thinking of using may very well have been used before, but a good plot is the key to making it your own.

A TRAIL OF CRUMBS

If you're anything like me, you'll hate plotting out your work. I'm extremely impatient when I'm writing and just want to leap in with all limbs flailing. But, just like jumping into a pool, if you do this, you'll go under. When embarking on any piece of writing it's always best to plot out events, even if it's just an outline – in other words, decide how you are going to tell your story step by step. It doesn't matter if you sketch this out roughly in your head, or fill a shelf of notepads with every single detail: without this map, you stand a very good chance of getting lost.

Learn more about posing the right questions and keeping up suspense in IDEA 37, *Buy one, get everything else free*.

Try another idea...

That isn't to say create a straitjacket for your characters that they have no way of escaping. As ever, your characters have to be the driving force behind your fiction, and no matter how well you delineate your plot they must be allowed a certain freedom to act, grow and develop naturally. When plotting, focus on your characters' feelings, emotions, reactions and thoughts as much as outside events. Don't just write 'character x races to character y's rescue'. Fill in the blanks, add notes about how the characters feel, what their fears and reservations are, whether they think they have the strength to rescue character y. This way, your plot line will develop more naturally, and you won't be tempted to steamroll past all of the important character depths when actually writing.

If you do decide to go for a generic plot, then think of ways to twist and subvert it. Readers will be expecting things to happen in a certain way, and by creating characters that do things differently, or by playing with a reader's expectations, you can create riveting surprises. By paying close attention to your characters and their inner drives, you can allow a plot to evolve that feels much more organic than one simply driven by events. Don't worry about learning your story by heart, just get to know your characters. Know their motives, know their passions, and a plot will form.

'There have been great societies that did not use the wheel, but there have been no societies that did not tell stories.'
URSULA K. LE GUIN

Defining idea...

How did it go?

Q **I've decided what story I want to use but – damn it! – someone's already done it. Is there any way of using the same story and making it unique?**

A *What will make your story unique is the strength and individuality of your characters, and the decisions you make linking and explaining the events. You have the imagination to make a standard story something unique to you. Make a skeleton plan of the main points of your story, then flesh it out with your character's actions and responses and the important causal links.*

Q **I've been told that plotting out your story precisely before you start writing is imperative. Isn't this a little too formal for something that's supposed to be creative?**

A *I've been told this too, but I always find that if you launch in and try to pin down everything that's going to happen in your novel it becomes restrictive when you're writing. Pencil in the key events, but let your characters provide the momentum and direction. It's important not to see your plot as a blueprint you are tied to. See it as a safety net, something you can fall back on if you get confused or lose your footing. Kazuo Ishiguro says 'I cannot start a story or chapter without knowing how it ends...Of course, it rarely ends that way.' When writing, plots are mercurial, ever changing, but as long as you have a firm grasp of your characters and their motivations it will always evolve into something interesting.*

35

Who's got the map?

Whether your plot is driving your work or following in the wake of your characters, there are certain techniques to getting from A to B without losing your passengers. Try the classical approach...

While every book is different, almost all classic plots go through a number of stages: beginnings, initiating event, quest, surprise, critical choice, climax, change and conclusion.

It's these stages that a reader subconsciously expects to find when reading a novel, and by omitting them you can risk losing your audience. Of course, you don't have to use the classical structure when writing – deviating from it can lead to some surprising and rewarding places – but it's always best to learn the rules before you go renegade.

GET THE BALL ROLLING

Every story has to have a beginning, an event that kick-starts everything else into motion, that disrupts the life of a character. This provocation – posh folk call this the 'initiating event' – can be a cataclysmic external change, like the breakout of

Here's an idea for you...

Analyse a piece of your own writing, or a plotline you've been working on. Is there an initiating event and a quest? What are the surprises, the critical choices, the climaxes? And do they bring about change? Looking at a plot along these lines can really help strengthen it.

war, or something internal, more personal to a character. It can be something so slight as to be almost unnoticeable.

It's this initiating event that gets the ball rolling, that sets events in motion. It's the thing that forces your characters out of their comfortable, everyday world – their once upon a time – into one that is strange and alien. When plotting out events, this initial provocation doesn't have to come straight away (look at the extended opening of *Sophie's Choice*), but it should happen fairly near the beginning. It's the conflict that will make your characters act, either by choice or by necessity, and it's their reactions to it that bring them to life, and make a plot worth following.

THE HOLY GRAIL

The effect of this initial event – this trigger – is to awaken your characters from an inactive state. In other words, it establishes a quest for them. Almost all classic stories can be read in this light: a character wants or needs something, and goes off to find it. Of course the plot for each new version of the story is different – they might need to find a lost love, be looking for meaning and self-revelation, seeking revenge, trying to get hold of some cash, growing from childhood to adulthood; it might even be laughable (think of poor old Don Quixote) – but the underlying story remains the same. A character's quest doesn't have to be external or physical – it could be a psychological or emotional journey. And the quest can change – although if your character starts out looking for power and ends up seeking love, the transition has to be believable.

SURRISE, SURPRISE

When plotting, it's vital to understand how the quest affects your character psychologically. You have to establish resistance for your character to fight against, obstacles they have to overcome. Why? Because paradoxically, the narrative surprises that prevent the character from enjoying a smooth journey to their goal are what pull the story forwards. Your characters' responses to these setbacks and conflicts – their 'critical choices' (posh folk, again) – are what keep readers interested. This resistance can be anything: another character, a global catastrophe, a domestic misunderstanding, a love interest who's not interested – but what it must do is provoke your character into making critical choices, and acting them out.

Resistance and conflict are bound together in fiction. Learn more about treating your characters mean in IDEA 18, *There may be trouble ahead.*

Try another idea...

HAPPILY EVER AFTER

The result of these actions is the climax. A man's father is murdered by his uncle (initiating event), the man decides to get revenge (critical choice) and murders his uncle (climax). The critical choice and the climax might occur almost in the same moment, or, as in *Hamlet*, they can take almost the entire length of the text to play out. A climax isn't always the final stage in a plot, however, and you can have more than one, but they have to lead to something, otherwise why did they occur? If a climax doesn't change a situation, then it's spectacle – action for the sake of action. Climaxes are the culmination of your characters' responses, and should change their emotional or physical status. If the surprises, critical choices and climaxes you use in your work don't lead to this change, readers may end up disappointed.

'When we read, we start at the beginning and continue until we reach the end. When we write, we start in the middle and fight our way out.'
VICKIE KARP, US poet

Defining idea...

Q **This formula sounds like magic. Should I use it to construct all of my stories from now on?**

A   *Whatever you do, don't assume that you can write a successful piece of fiction simply by following a classical pattern. There are no plot machines that can make an instant work of literature – every novel is unique, much greater than the sum of its parts. Use the classical structure to outline your plot, and to give you a clearer sense of where you are, but remember that it's your writing, and your individual creative touch that will make it work. This structure can be more useful as a checklist to come back to when you're struggling to keep a plot moving.*

Q **As my partner tells me, I'm not always the most organised of people. Do I have to start writing from the beginning and work chronologically, or can I keep to my own time?**

A   *I usually start at the beginning of a novel and work forwards (it feels more natural for me, although I always go back and change things when I'm editing). A great many writers throw chronology out the window, however, and write a scene here, a scene there and sew the patchwork together when they're ready. But be warned: if you take this latter approach, it can be difficult to keep track of the pace and emotional evolution of your novel, and you must always ensure that the joins between each scene are seamless.*

36

All good things come in threes

Tackling the intricacies of script plotting in a single chapter is like trying to squeeze Arnold Schwarzenegger into a romper suit. But try these useful pointers to keep things moving in the right direction.

When you're writing a screenplay, you have to learn to be tight. Not tight in the Scrooge sense, but in terms of keeping close control of the dramatic structure of your story and script.

There are two cardinal sins of screenplay writing. The first is to forget about structure, to try and make it resemble real life as closely as possible. The result: a screenplay that ends up as uneventful and understructured as, well, real life. The second is an emphasis on style over content. The result: an overstructured, over-complex plot with no depth. All the script readers I know say that the classic three-act linear structure is the path to success. Hey, it's worked since Aristotle!

Here's an idea for you... **Think of how you are planning to end your story, the final climax. Then plot out the opening act. Does it set the story in motion, and propel it towards your finale? Does it establish your protagonist and set the scene? Does it pose a problem that she must confront and overcome, and does it indicate what the story is going to be about? With enough practice, you'll be following the structure without even noticing it any more.**

WALKING THE TIGHTROPE

See your screenplay as a series of breakdowns based around what you consider to be the most dramatic moments. The most obvious breakdown is the most general one, into acts 1, 2 and 3, which are then broken down into sequences and scenes. This structure is your blueprint, the frame around which you can mould your action and dialogue. Don't feel you have to force your baby into this overarching structure – it's just a mechanism to help you tell your story more effectively.

COMMERCIAL BREAKDOWN

The first act (which should take up around a quarter of the total screenplay) is the space you have to set the scene. It's where you establish your script's heartbeat. You introduce the main characters and their worlds, you establish what the story will be about and set the tone, you prime the tensions, you set the timescale. Script readers often say that they can gauge a script's quality on the first few pages, so this is your chance to shine. Grab their attention with a hook, pull them into your story. This can be spectacular (think *Swordfish*), or subtle (*Good Will Hunting*), but it must pique the reader's interest. This initiating event is what kick-starts the move towards a final climax. At the end of act 1 there should be another climactic event: something that increases the stakes, increases momentum, builds tension and propels the story forwards, keeping the viewer hooked.

WHO'S FOR SECONDS?

Check out IDEA 38, *Coming over all emotional*, for ways to increase the power of a script.

Try another idea...

The second act (which should take a whopping half of the total screenplay) is your main story. You've kicked things into motion with the events of act 1. Now you show how it all develops. Here's your chance to explore how your characters respond to the inciting incident, the way they progress towards their final goal. It's best to see this act as two halves: to keep things interesting, midway through the second act the character usually faces a setback. This is usually the point of no return, their moment of complete commitment. With more at risk, the tension builds, the focus narrows, and your characters become more clearly defined through their actions. At the end of this act comes the moment of truth, the second climactic event where they meet an obstacle that threatens to defeat them. With a clearer sense of who they are and what they must do, your characters are ready for the final showdown of act 3.

AN EXPLOSIVE CLIMAX

Act 3 (which, as the mathematicians among you will have deduced, should take up the last quarter of the total screenplay) should accelerate towards a strong final climax, where a character faces the biggest obstacle of all. Everything in a screenplay should be pointing towards this final goal, moving the script inexorably towards it – it's for a good reason that people in the business say screenplays are written backwards. Your character may finish successfully, or fail, but whether good or bad, make the ending believable and satisfying.

Defining idea...

'The "numbers" you get on many courses or in various books should be used to develop your storytelling instincts, to validate your guesses and intuitions, and then forget them. Learn them, them throw them away.'
DAVID WEBB PEOPLES, screenwriter

How did
it go?

Q **Trying to plot the events of my screenplay is like trying to herd cats! Are there any useful ways of keeping things under control when plotting?**

A *One excellent technique to try is to plan out your outline on cards, scene by scene. Use pieces of paper 7.5 cm tall by 12.5 cm wide, each representing a scene from your film. On each, make brief notes about what happens, including how it starts and ends. When you've filled them out, you have an extremely strong visual pattern of your script in front of you. Use this to get an idea of its structure, its pacing, and whether you need to add or remove anything.*

Q **And trying to fit my flowing story into a set formula is like trying to cram a five year old into his least favourite jumper. What can I do?**

A *Most importantly, don't force it. It's probable that you can break down your existing story into stages based on your characters' conflicts, actions and state of mind. Try and think of every scene as a burst of energy, each of which grips the viewers' interest and pulls them along towards a final climax. Keeping viewers hooked is the priority.*

Q **Is this the only structure to work with?**

A *Not at all. You can have two acts, or four or five acts. But remember, the key turning points and climaxes should remain in the same place (relative to the number of acts) if the format is to work. There are plenty of other templates to use as a point of reference: read Joseph Campbell's* The Hero With a Thousand Faces *for another commonly used template (this one was the basis for* Star Wars*).*

37

Buy one, get everything else free

Having a clear idea of where your work is heading is all well and good, but remember: readers don't like a giveaway, so keep them guessing by plotting cleverly.

Getting the reader to turn page after page is the most important concern for a writer, and the best way to arrest their attention is by raising questions and delaying the answers.

If you pose an intriguing enough question at the beginning of a piece of writing a reader will charge through a thousand pages or more to find out what happens – just look at *The Lord of the Rings*.

MAKING SENSE

Plot, especially in a novel, is like a treasure map. As a writer, you're guaranteeing to a reader that the instructions you give them will lead them through the dark forest to the golden doubloons at the end – it's a guarantee that you're sending them in the right direction, and that whatever lies at the end is worth the trip. If the map

Here's an idea for you...

Try visualising your plotline as an electrocardiogram – the pattern of your heartbeat represented as a line. Plot events roughly along this line. Think about what elements of the plot will create questions that the reader will desperately want to see resolved. Each time a question is raised, mark a heartbeat on your plotline, and keep the line waving until it is resolved. During the quiet parts, keep the line flat. If your cardiogram is flatlining, boredom could be setting in. If it resembles the ocean during a hurricane, you may be overdoing it.

you provide doesn't meet these two requirements, the readers will lose their way, and you'll lose their trust.

But it's a little more complicated than this. Readers aren't just looking for a final payoff – they don't want freebies. If people were after a quick resolution, all stories would be two pages long: a beginning, then straight away a conclusion. Or readers would skip to the last page of a novel as soon as they'd finished the first. The map you provide has to be one that takes the reader on a number of adventures, that builds up their suspense and relieves it bit by bit on the journey to the end. Readers like to be teased. They want to get to the end of a novel (how many times have you cursed yourself for not being able to read fast enough to find out what happens at the end of a book?) but they also want to feel they've got something from the whole experience, not just the resolution.

A REAL PAGE TURNER

In order to create tension in a plot, to keep readers turning those pages, you need to ask questions and hold back the answers. In most texts, the initiating event poses the big question: readers want to know how a character is going to react, and what the outcome will be. If the uncertainty you create at the beginning of the book is exciting enough, they'll keep reading until they get to the end, until the question is resolved.

Look at IDEA 38, *Coming over all emotional*, for ways to make people tense and emotional – in a good way.

Try another idea...

For some, though, the thought of slogging through an entire novel for a final resolution is daunting, so keep up the tension by posing smaller questions in each chapter. Remember, each problem or obstacle you pose for a character is a question raised – every challenge you set a character creates an uncertainty in the reader: will they make it out of this one? Keep your readers hooked by holding back the answer, and posing another question as soon as the previous one is resolved. You can do this at the start of the chapter, or you can end chapters with a cliffhanger, but either way the reader is propelled forwards by their need to find out what happens next. Many thriller writers have got this down to a fine art.

TRAVEL WATCH

Whether you're creating a plot from an outline, or leaving it to the actions of your characters, you should be aiming to show how life is a great deal more complicated than a simple story. And in order to do this, you don't just want to be showing events themselves, you need to focus on how they shape your characters. Plot is a journey, sometimes physically but always emotionally and psychologically. Central characters need to change in the course of a plot: when they arrive at point B they can be anywhere – happier, sadder, richer, poorer, deader – as long as they are not still at point A. Somewhere between each uncertainty and each resolution, your characters change, they evolve. Without this change, for better or for worse, readers will find it hard to empathise with your characters.

'Make 'em laugh; make 'em cry; make 'em wait.'
CHARLES READE, UK novelist

Defining idea...

165

Q My plot electrocardiogram currently resembles the Great Hungarian Plain. How should I use the timing of my questions and answers to change the pace of my writing?

A *Creating uncertainties is like injecting nitrous oxide into your car's engine. If readers really care about your characters they'll read as quickly as they humanly can in order to find out how a complication resolves itself, only pausing for a rest when they know what's happened. Turning to thrillers again, books like* The Da Vinci Code *pose an uncertainty virtually at the end of every chapter, so you end up being unable to put the book down even when you're supposed to be working. Remember, though, readers need a break every now and again.*

Q What's the difference between a suspense plot and a mystery plot?

A *In short, these are the two types of narrative question you can ask: with mystery it's 'what happened?' With suspense it's 'what happens next?' They both involve an initiating event, although with mystery the plot works backwards, trying to solve a puzzle.*

Q I am an artiste, and I'm focusing on creating a brilliant style, so does my plot really matter?

A *It shouldn't matter how brilliant your style is. To create an enjoyable piece of writing you have to raise questions of some sort and delay their answer. If you simply write a piece of brilliant prose, abandoning plot for style, you can risk sending your readers to sleep.*

38

Coming over all emotional

How can you, the screenwriter, make sure your audience gets emotionally involved with on-screen events? Hooking viewers is like catching fish – you've just got to find the right bait.

If you know what to put on the end of the line — if you know what to include and what to leave out of a script — you can lead an audience anywhere you like.

Characters are what hook movie audiences, but only characters that are in motion – that are motivated. At the beginning of a story, a character's drives are based on his background – physical and emotional. During the course of the story, these motivations will be transformed by the events of your plot – characters will encounter problems, form new goals and change as a result. This tends to follow a certain pattern: problem – goal – action to achieve the goal – crisis and a setback – climax and point of change. This pattern doesn't simply govern the entire screenplay, it should also drive every act.

The initial motivation for a character usually comes from his history – he often finds himself in a personal crisis, whether or not he actually realises it. This crisis

Here's an idea for you...

It's vital to get the pacing right, the flow of highs and lows, action and pauses. You need to vary the moments of excitement. It's good to think about the pace of your screenplay when you're plotting it out – deciding what kind of pace it will have early on will help you keep the tension throughout.

unsettles his position, makes a change of direction extremely likely and allows you to kick-start the script. If you throw an inciting incident at a character in personal crisis your story will explode into life, rather than relying on a push. The crisis, the inciting incident and the character's motivation must be extremely clear – you've only got a couple of hours to tell your story, and viewers need as many clues as possible to understand what's going on.

NEWTON'S LAWS

In order to make a story move forwards it needs a push. OK, Newton didn't exactly say that, but you can apply his laws to writing. Movement and momentum are achieved by building tension, which is generated when an audience hopes (or fears) that something is about to happen to the characters. There are numerous ways of achieving tension and momentum, but they all revolve around anticipation and suspense.

In order to pull the audience through your story, you need anticipation: the thought that something is going to happen. This causes an audience to think ahead, to anticipate the end result and therefore to desperately will the story to move forwards as quickly as possible to find out if they're right. By providing just enough information to allow an audience to think ahead (wondering what or when something will happen), but withholding the answers until later on, you'll keep them hooked right through the film. Whether you stay faithful to that anticipation, or whether you deviate from it and create a surprise, is up to you – just never leave an anticipated event unresolved.

CRUEL TO BE KIND

If you want to be cruel, keep your audience in a state of suspense by making the outcome of an event uncertain. If the audience really doesn't know how a situation will resolve, they won't take their eyes off the screen until it has played out. Suspense can work within a single scene, or it can be played out across the entire film. A character's goals, and what she does to reach them, determine the level of suspense: if the goals are too easy, there will be no uncertainty and therefore no suspense. With enough challenges and difficulties, the tension becomes unbearable. In order to make the most of suspense, it's vital that the audience has a clear idea of a character's goal and the difficulties she faces trying to achieve it.

Setting up the pace of your screenplay is always connected to how you structure it. See IDEA 36, *All good things come in threes*, for notes on plotting.

Try another idea...

BIGGER RISKS

Another way to keep audiences hooked is by increasing the stakes throughout your script. If the risk is increased, so is a character's state of jeopardy, and therefore also the audience's capacity for empathising with her. The stakes must be raised higher as the story progresses – they can't be allowed to decrease towards the end. Remember, though, getting your character right is paramount to making this work. If your audience doesn't care what happens to a protagonist, there won't be any tension even if the stakes go through the roof.

'A character's dreams are most important because I think almost always what their dreams are will help you motivate the story. It's something they want.'
LAWRENCE KONNER, screenwriter

Defining idea...

Q **I want to send people's blood pressure through the roof. Are there any other ways of increasing tension?**

A *In order to get the most from an action scene, or a moment of intense emotional drama, precede it with a scene of relief and tranquillity. This will cause the audience to drop their guard, making the drama even more engaging.*

Q **Can I manipulate the audience's emotions simply by showing the same feelings in a character?**

A *It's a little more complicated than this. If you show an actor looking happy, it doesn't necessarily mean your audience will feel happy too. Audiences empathise with characters with whom they identify, so it's the way you manipulate your characters, the situations you put them in and the way they react, that will make your viewers laugh or cry.*

Q **Is it important that my character's goal is made explicit? Can't I just leave it to the audience's imagination?**

A *Your protagonist's goal is their most important motivation, and therefore the driving force of the film. It's this that forces them into conflict, the resistance that powers the film towards the final climax. If this goal isn't clear to an audience, your character's motivation may not be clear, and as a result her actions will lack meaning and definition. If an audience doesn't know what motivates a character, or what she's aiming for, they won't get a true sense of the difficulties she's facing – and without this knowledge, there can be very little suspense and drama.*

39

Subletting your story

Subplots may seem like unnecessary baggage, but they're vital to creating a believable and engaging story.

A single storyline doesn't provide enough flesh to sustain an entire novel or film, and will prevent your characters from gaining depth or the plot from developing meaning. Let's start subletting...

Subplots are subsidiary storylines that run alongside, and are linked to, the main plot. It's up to you how many subplots you decide to set up and string along: television drama usually has one subplot, motion pictures have a main plot, a subplot and three or four minor subplots, and novels can have several subplots developed to different levels. There are two main rules, though: they shouldn't be necessary to the plot – if you took them away, the storyline shouldn't become a mess; but they should always inform and feed into your main plot, contributing meaning to it.

In novels and screenplays, the way you move in and out of your plot and your subplot will determine how much momentum your story generates. If your subplots

Here's an idea for you...

Make a grid on a large piece of paper, with the timescale of your novel running along the top and the various subplots running down the side. Using a different coloured pen for each subplot write down what's going on in each strand at each point in the story. Then use a bright marker to circle those elements of each plot that you think will contribute most to pace and meaning. This visual planning will help you work out how your subplots relate to your main story.

aren't linked by action or by theme your story won't seem grounded, and readers will find it hard to work out where to invest most of their attention. If you jump back and forth between subplots too frequently, or leave extended periods of time between visiting each subplot, your story will stop and start, unable to build up any momentum and ultimately failing to hold a reader's interest. It may take some time to work out how many subplots you need, and where exactly to integrate them into the main action, but it's well worth some careful planning to avoid confusion.

THE FOURTH DIMENSION

If subplots aren't necessary to the main story, I hear you ask, then why should we bother with them? Well, there are a number of reasons. The most important of these is to 'fill out' the main plot, to ensure that it's multi-dimensional, not flat. Fiction and film can risk becoming an oversimplified version of events: they are life neatened up, with the boring stuff cut away. Limited to a single main plot, characters can risk becoming wooden, mechanical – we only see them in the light of the story, we don't see them from other angles. It's like looking at a photograph: we can't see the subtle nuances, the full perspective. Subplots enable this flattened plot to fill out. The minor characters that make up the subplots allow a reader to see the main characters and the main plot from various alternative angles, giving them substance and depth. Subplots also help to pace the main plot, preventing it from racing along frantically to a premature climax. Use a subplot to add obstacles to the hero's quest and complicate their path to achieving their goals – it will help build tension and ensure that the story doesn't slide to an unfulfilling conclusion after fifty pages.

All of your characters need plot lines of their own. Learn more about delving into a character's past in IDEA 18, *There may be trouble ahead.*

Try another idea...

ARE YOU WITH ME OR NOT?

Subplots can be related to the main plot in a number of ways. The first of these is complementary: it resonates with the main plot, basically confirming our knowledge and opinions of the characters and their actions. Whether or not a subplot resonates with the action of the main plot, it should always resonate with the theme of a novel or screenplay, reinforcing or throwing new light on the underlying message of the text. Alternatively, a subplot can be contradictory to the main plot, moving against the action and ideas. In some films and novels, subplots are used to complicate the main plot, often by throwing in a love interest that ups the stakes or alters a character's motives. Lastly, a subplot can act as a set-up plot, keeping the audience engaged until the main plot begins.

'The object of the novelist is to keep the reader entirely oblivious of the fact that the author exists – even of the fact he is reading a book.'
FORD MADOX FORD

Defining idea...

How did
it go?

Q **I'm struggling to balance the subplots and the main plot. The subplot keeps getting out of control! Can't I just have two main plots?**

A *It is possible, but it can be difficult to strike the right balance. If you develop a subplot too much it risks becoming a main plot, with its own developmental arc and a need for a climax and resolution. With two main plots in a text competing for dominance a reader may become confused, or you may lose the sense of urgency that you're trying to convey in each narrative strand. It's possible to have a multiple-plotted movie or novel, but you run the risk of losing focus. You've been warned!*

Q **My partner read my script and said he couldn't tell the difference between the plots. OK he's a bit of a bonehead and I have been trying to be subtle, but should I make the distinction more obvious?**

A *Perhaps you should get a second opinion! In good films and books, you tend not to notice that there are several different strands evolving at once because they are so well integrated, and the theme throughout each is so strong that it bonds them tightly and seamlessly. If one subplot is less developed than the others, is running at a significantly faster or slower pace, or has a different tone, then you'll probably end up frustrating your readers.*

40

Yakety yak, don't talk back

Ah, we get to it at last, the great debate. Rhyme. Sometimes it's in, sometimes it's just so passé; some people consider it compulsory, others unnecessary. Let's look at the reasons for rhyme.

Like it or not, rhyme is intimately linked with poetry, and can help bring shape and meaning to an otherwise shambolic poem. But it can also become repetitive, predictable and just downright ridiculous.

Rhyme is one of the most effective ways of holding a poem together and giving it strength. Used cleverly, rhyme is like the tumblers falling into place, each rhyme gives that satisfying click as the words link up – even if you're tackling difficult concepts, using rhyme gives the impression of order, harmony and control.

CAT/HAT, THOUGHT/FOUGHT, CHIMNEY, UM...

English isn't always an easy language to rhyme in (just try and find a suitable rhyme for 'chimney' or 'orange'), but see this as an advantage. Rhyming in Italian or

Here's an idea for you... **Try a sonnet. Pick the rhyming words first, without thinking about a subject. Use this as a framework and fill it out, working with whatever theme or subject suggests itself. Don't worry about the number of words or syllables per line, just focus on the rhymes. Now try another sonnet, but pick your subject matter, and then try and rhyme – aim to get the rhymes to feel as natural as possible.**

French is a little too easy, and because of this, predictable. And when you're deciding on rhymes for a poem, the last thing you want to be is clichéd. Yes, there are plenty of rhymes for puck, but don't fall into the trap of going for the easy option – nothing is more likely to send the reader into a coma than a highly predictable rhyme scheme.

Likewise, never make the mistake of choosing words solely for their rhyme. More often than not, you risk compromising a line's meaning by doing so. I'm friendly with a group of performance poets who almost always use rhyme in their work. When I asked them their secret, they all sheepishly held up their rhyming dictionaries. Don't laugh – if you're thinking of using rhymes, getting yourself one of these can really help.

BE TRADITIONAL

If you want to try something tricky, using a traditional form for your poetry can really help you get to grips with rhyme. One of the most popular forms for experimentation is the fourteen-line Petrarchan sonnet, with the rhyme scheme abba abba cde cde (no, that's not an obscure reference to a Swedish pop group, but the easy way of noting a rhyme scheme: with lines in a verse represented by the same letter employing the same rhyme). It may seem rather limited, but it's the challenge of trying to fit the chaos of experience into such an ordered mould that many find so attractive – it can really help you focus on what you're trying to say.

BE ORIGINAL

But rhyming doesn't have to equate to the sonnet, the limerick or the couplet. Rhyme schemes can be complex, hidden to all but the subconscious mind of the reader. When rhyming, try to make your structure as unpredictable and surprising as possible. Don't simply end every line with a rhyme and a pause, like the heroic couplet. Instead, break up a predictable structure by allowing the sense of one line to run on to the next, meaning it's not just the last word in a sentence that rhymes. Using this technique – technically referred to as enjambement – can enable you to keep up a rhyme scheme without making your poem too predictable.

Learn more about the music of poetry in IDEA 8, *When the rhythm starts to play.*

Try another idea...

DON'T STOP THERE

And don't just stop with full rhymes. Rhyming is personal to each poem: it's up to you how far you stretch the sound of a word. You can rhyme the vowels of a word (crowd, bough), or try using the consonants (groaned, groined). You can use rhymes involving polysyllables, such as 'histories' and 'mysteries'; but you don't have to stick to words of the same length: there's nothing to stop you rhyming 'indisputable' with 'bull'. Use bad rhymes if you want to draw attention to something, use internal rhymes to help break up a repetitive section of a poem, rhyme a stressed word with an unstressed word, or rhyme a word with itself. It really is up to you.

'Anybody can write the first line of a poem, but it is a very difficult task to make the second line rhyme with the first.'
MARK TWAIN

Defining idea...

179

How did it go?

Q **I love the idea of rhyming but I'm struggling to find words that match up. Is there a technique to finding the right rhyme or do I have to adopt a leprechaun that will sing rhyming words at me all day long?**

A *Finding the right rhyme often comes down to perseverance and luck. The important thing to remember is to always ask yourself how a rhyme contributes to the overall meaning and effect of the poem. If you're stuck for an explanation, it might be worth a rethink. When practising with rhyme, the key is to try and make an unnatural linguistic device sound natural.*

Q **Should I be force-feeding my rhyme a high-fibre diet to make sure it's regular?**

A *Not at all. You can use rhymes that are looser than the bowels of a dysentery sufferer. Stitching a poem together with a loose rhyme scheme can make it seem natural or colloquial whilst also hinting at the structure underneath.*

Q **Reading back through some of my poetry, I've used some rhymes without even meaning to. Am I just exceptionally clever or could this be a bad thing?**

A *If you accidentally use rhyming words in your unrhymed poetry, especially at the end of lines that are next to one another, the result can be confusing. Readers may assume you're trying to draw attention to something, or wonder why only a few lines are linked by rhyme.*

41

Size doesn't matter

Short stories take a moment in time selected from a much larger narrative, compress characters and meaning into a tiny space and (hopefully) create something intense and beautiful.

Ask any writer, and they'll tell you that short stories are one of the most challenging techniques to get right. Yet strangely enough, most beginners undertake this form before any other.

It can be all too easy to write a bad short story (believe me, I've penned some real stinkers), but with enough practice not only will you craft some wonderful short fiction, you'll also develop many of the techniques you need to be able to write convincing novels.

DOING A LINFORD

If novel writing is like running a marathon, then a short story is a sprint. There's less distance to travel but you've got to find that special something to get you from start to finish as dynamically as possible. Whether these successful stories are dramatic

Here's an idea for you...

Pick a character and a conflict, and try and write a convincing and engaging short story in 1,000 words or less. Don't count the words as you write: pen what you think is 1,000 words then edit down if you're over. Now try writing the same story in 100 words or less. The choices you make about which bits to cut and which bits to save will help you learn what it is about a short story that makes it successful.

(think Edgar Allan Poe) or subtle (look at the beautifully crafted tales of Anton Chekhov, Katherine Mansfield or Raymond Carver), the secret is in portraying realistic characters and making the reader care about what happens to them – as much as they would characters in a novel.

CAKE BAKING

Baking a successful short story needs careful consideration of its ingredients. Most short stories develop from an idea, a flash of inspiration from real life or from something you've read or watched on television. One of my short stories was born while watching a TV programme about the world's worst jobs. One man was a body fisherman – somebody who dredged human bodies from the Ganges after they had been laid to rest. It was such a shocking and unusual way of life that I felt compelled to write a story about it.

Of course a short story could just as easily originate from a character, one you're experimenting with or who really piques your interest. Whatever the events of your story, they have to excite you, and have to involve realistic, rounded characters. In short fiction, try to introduce your character as close to the opening of the story as possible – if you delay, you risk losing readers. There isn't a hell of a lot of space to do this, but one way to keep in control is to keep things simple – stick to one main character throughout, either letting them narrate or maintaining a limited third-person outlook, keep to a fairly short time span, and try not to lose focus by introducing unnecessary characters or plot lines.

CONFLICT ZONE

Another vital ingredient of the short story is conflict. Characters must be faced with a problem at the outset. Without this 'bait' early on readers probably won't bite. Just remember, though, that conflict doesn't have to be grand – most successful short stories are attractive because they involve conflict on a very subtle and personal level.

Look at IDEAS 14, 15 and 18 for ways to make your characters come alive, even if it's only for a 1,000 words.

Try another idea…

If you create realistic characters that engage a reader's interest, then any problem you create, however small, will build up a sense of anxiety, an unbearable suspense. If people care about a character, they will always want to know what happens to them, even if it's just waiting to see if they decide to pick up the phone.

KEEPING IT TOGETHER

Short stories have to be tight or they risk becoming, well, long stories. It's often best to plot out a rough outline of what's going to happen, scene by scene, to stop your story unravelling. But even if you're not sure exactly what's going to happen, remember to constantly question your motives for including a certain description or scene. If your ideas and characters are strong enough, you should feel the plot tugging in one certain direction, with each scene suggesting the one that follows.

Defining idea…

'A short story occurs in the imaginative sense. To write one is to express from a situation in the exterior or interior world the life-giving drop – sweat, tear, semen, saliva – that will spread in intensity on the page; burn a hole in it.'
NADINE GORDIMER

How did it go?

Q   How short is short?

A   There's no divine code of length when it comes to short stories. They can be as small as 100 words (common in competitions) or longer than 5,000 words, but 1,0000–2,000 words is common. Obviously, if you're gearing your story towards a certain market or competition, always check their word limit – it's not worth ruining your chances because you're reluctant to edit. Saying that, I hate the thought of amputating my story or stretching it to fit a set regulation. It always reminds me of the Greek myth of Procrustes – who either stretched his guests or chopped off their legs depending on whether they were too long or too short for his bed. Just as with his poor victims, this manipulation of length can be fatal.

Q   Surely short stories are so short they shouldn't need such a classical structure? Crikey, that was a bit of a tongue twister!

A   Even short stories must have a beginning (where the characters, scene and problems are introduced), a middle (where the action is developed and the reader becomes increasingly intrigued by events) and an end (a resolution). It's up to you how the story ends. Some readers believe a short story won't work unless there's a twist at the end. This is a fairly restrictive view, but there should be change of some kind by the time the story finishes – there doesn't have to be a shocking twist, but an ending should be surprising, even if it's just a change in a character's outlook.

42

Show and tell

The first commandment of writing: show, don't tell. By showing you're letting the reader project something of their own experience into the writing. Showing is sharing – always the nice thing to do.

What would be more exciting: visiting Disneyworld and riding on every roller coaster twelve times, or listening to a friend going on about when they visited Disneyworld and rode every roller coaster twelve times?

Unless you really hate riding roller coasters, I'd guess the actual experience would be more exciting than hearing about it from somebody else. The same applies to writing, whether prose, poetry or drama: show, don't tell.

SDT

If we were to conduct a survey into what words most frequently appeared in workshops and creative writing seminars, we'd probably end up with 'show', 'don't' and 'tell'. It's so common a phrase now it even has its own abbreviation. But why

Here's an idea for you... **Try writing about your own personal hell (poetry, prose or drama, it's up to you), or a time when you were absolutely terrified. First, tell your reader about it through description and abstract emotion. Next, show it, describe how it felt, try to convey the horror of the experience, try to transport your readers. I don't think I'll need to ask you which will be the most evocative.**

should we SDT? Aren't writers supposed to tell stories? Yes, but we want to make readers feel like they are part of our literary world; to become immersed in our text, not just think they're hearing it from an old man at the bus stop.

When writing, we want to transport readers, convince them that this world of words is the real thing: we don't just want to tell them that the heroine is in danger, we want to make the reader feel that danger, hear her pounding heart, sense the killer's breath on the back of her neck, try and fight the panic of imminent danger. People don't always believe what they're told, but they do believe the evidence of their own senses. Likewise, people don't always engage emotionally with the characters they hear about in stories, but if they're put in that person's shoes, they can't help but empathise. That's where SDT kicks in.

UNDERWRITING...

No, it's not an insurance term: it's telling when you really should be showing. If you start explaining to the reader something that you should be dramatising, you're not giving a scene the impact it should have: 'She wanted to tell him how much she loved him' – yawn! And it doesn't help if you resort to abstract terms either: telling your reader that a character is 'madly and deeply in love' is no substitute for actually showing how that person feels: 'She was trembling, her stomach in knots. She wanted to feel his arms around her, his fingers on her spine. She wanted to fold her body into his, so whenever he went away next she'd always be there – warm, ready.'

How exactly do you show something on the page? Look at IDEA 19, *It's alive!*, for some pointers.

Try another idea…

You have to set your imagination to work full time to show things in a way that is moving and believable. Yes, telling is much easier, but if you can't invest your words with any humanity or any depth, if you just tell the story from a detached viewpoint, you risk a reader shutting off and thinking about what they're going to make for dinner, or what kind of bathroom cleaner to buy next.

HAVE FAITH

By telling, you're assuming a reader needs things spelt out as simply as possible. You have to have faith in your reader's imagination: don't try and explain everything in a scene, credit a reader with enough creative power to fill in the blanks, to contribute something of her own experience. To truly make readers feel like they've been transported to your world, you need to let them bring part of their own life to the text: telling everything – setting, character, plot – in minute detail denies them this and makes the text the author's empire, a world that leaves no room for them. Showing allows readers to project part of their own experience into the story – it becomes a story for them, rather than one simply told to them.

'Don't tell me the moon is shining; show me the glint of light on broken glass.'
ANTON CHEKHOV

Defining idea…

How did it go?

Q OK, SDT. It sounds like something people need to go to a clinic for but aside from that it seems to be making my writing more powerful. So it's always best to show, rather then tell, right?

A There are exceptions to the rule. (Aren't there always?) You don't want to show everything in a piece of writing, or else it may become a tad tedious. Many of the stories and poems I read, especially those by younger writers, show absolutely everything from the word go. We see the protagonist walk down the street, into the shop, buy a chocolate bar, undo the wrapper, eat it, go home, put the kettle on... That's an exaggeration, but you get the idea: if you show too much, things get silly.

Q Then how do I know when to show and when to tell?

A From personal experience, I'd say it's easier to pin down where you should have shown and not told (or vice-versa) retrospectively. When reading through your work, look out for moments when your choice of narrative strategy causes a jolt – a moment where you're suddenly aware of the text, not the events within. Chances are it will either be a result of underwriting or, more rarely, showing too much. If in doubt, try rewriting and either showing or telling, whichever you didn't choose before. You should find it helps keep the text alive.

43

The big read

It will be hard, it may even be nasty, but you have to re–read your work in order to improve it. Get your 'built-in shit detector' ready.

So, it's finally finished. Your magnum opus has been saved, printed and now sits behemoth-like on your desk lapping up more pride and attention than a newborn baby.

You have, after a labour of weeks, months, maybe years, given birth. And just like any parent, you see that manuscript as the sheer epitome of perfection. But is it? There's only one way to be sure, and whilst it is effective, it isn't always easy...

BITING THE BULLET

Anybody with writers for friends will smile knowingly whenever they hear H. G. Wells' statement that 'no passion in the world is greater than the passion to alter someone else's draft'. Every writer has a built-in editor, a Samaritan if you like, that wants to bandage scrappy dialogue or amputate unwanted adjectives in any text they read. Unfortunately, however, this Samaritan usually makes itself most apparent when you are reading drafts written by friends – a confrontation which

Here's an idea for you...

If you're going over a piece that you've just written, there are no surprises, as you know exactly how and why something is about to happen. You're using your memory more than your critical skills. But if you put your manuscript under your bed or in your wardrobe for a few months, rereading it is almost like launching into a book by a stranger. Not only will it help you pick out renegade words and sentences that don't belong, but you may also spot vital (and potentially embarrassing) flaws in character or plot that weren't visible close up.

can lead to anything from sulky arguments to full-blown family feuds. Just as unfortunately, this benevolent internal editor rarely makes an appearance when it is most needed – when you are reading your own work.

OBJECTION!

'But I do read my own work!' I can hear you cry, and yes, that's exactly what I argued when given the same advice. Practically all writers read their own work, but only a few actually see their own work. What's the difference? It's like sailors who spend their entire life on the ocean – they get so used to the movements of their boat that after a while they don't even notice it, and the only time they can see it is when they step on to dry land. Re-reading your work can pose the same symptoms. You are so familiar with what's on the page that although you're reading through it, you're not seeing it, and the more you read it back, the more invisible it becomes. In order to awaken the internal editor, in order to see your work as everybody else will, you need to step off the boat.

A BUILT-IN SHIT DETECTOR

Ernest Hemmingway once famously said that 'the most essential gift for a good writer is a built-in, shock-proof shit detector. This is the writer's radar, and all good writers should have it.' Easily said, but actually extremely difficult to put into practice when reading your own precious words. Each sentence, each paragraph, is important to you because you remember writing it, and because you understand what it means to you. But it's easy to fall in love with your words for this very reason, and it's one of the biggest pitfalls of writing.

What Hemmingway means, and what your internal editor has to learn to do, is try to uncover how your writing will look to an outsider – in other words, to a reader. By distancing yourself from your own words, by reading them, as it were, from dry land, it is far easier to detect those clumsy sentences that have sneaked through quality control, those adjectives that have crashed the party, or even those secondary characters that have inexplicably returned from the dead. Learning to view your work as a reader would (and no, I don't mean like your mum), is the only way to engage the all-important shit detector, and ensure that your work will appeal to those who aren't, well; you.

Try another idea…

It's not easy to edit while you write, but there are methods of damage limitation that will make the editing process much easier. See IDEA 11, *A sensuous, transcendent, sublime chapter*, for ways to stop your text getting out of hand.

Defining idea…

'*I love being a writer. It's the paperwork I can't stand.*'
PETER DE VRIES, US editor and novelist

191

How did it go?

Q   I can't wait six months before I read my book. What if somebody else publishes something similar in the meantime and everybody thinks I'm copying?

A   *Your paranoia seems to be developing nicely, I see! Try reading your work out aloud to yourself (like Graham Greene did), or better yet, get somebody else to read it to you. It's surprising just how different your words will sound when they enter through the ears instead of the eyes.*

Q   I'm a bit nervous about leaving all the re–reading until the work is finished. Can I take a few sneaky peaks along the way?

A   *Reading through a little of what you've written before you begin writing is important. It can also be time consuming, and you don't want to spend three hours re-reading then 30 minutes writing each time you sit down to work. Set yourself a fixed number of pages to read before you start writing. This will help you get back into the pace, rhythm and character of your work.*

Q   What happens if I re-read my work and hate it? What if it isn't as good as I remember it? What if it makes me nauseous? I'd rather just assume it is OK.

A   *All writers have thought like this at one point, but the ones with courage push the boat out (yes, another nautical metaphor) and read, read, read. Don't worry if you don't like what you see – it's good that you caught it, because if you don't like it, it's unlikely that your readers will. See this as an opportunity to polish off your raw work.*

44

Armageddon

People either avoid editing altogether or try and squeeze it in at the most inopportune moment – when writing. To get the most from your internal editor, stop it barging in and ask it to make an appointment.

Your creative self, the part you call 'writer', wants to be let off the leash. It wants to run wild, be spontaneous and do nothing but flick two fingers up at the authorities in your brain.

But your organised self, the editor within, wants to keep control. Like Big Brother it watches everything and sends in the thought police if you're getting out of hand. And for most creative people, Room 101 is simply the fear that what they're writing is no good. Learn to harness – not fight – your editor for the best way to creative freedom.

CAGE WARS

The battle between the writer and the editor within isn't a one-off, end-of-season, championship bout, it's an ongoing, never-ending slagging match that begins as soon as you pick up a pen. When writing, it's important to let your creative side have free rein to explore and experiment. It doesn't matter if what you're writing

Here's an idea for you...

Plan your writing time so you know when you're wearing the creative hat and when you're donning your editor's cap. Your creative flow will have more power and your editor can step back knowing it will take the wheel later on. Found a trial audience? Then bite the bullet and quiz them: do you empathise with the characters? Can you follow the plot? Did the dialogue make you cringe? Was it worth reading? Get honest answers and use them.

isn't prize-winning material, it's the initial stream, the first draft, a creative splurge. If you start to edit during this creative phase, you'll only end up stalling, time after time. You can't stop writing and start nit-picking, then expect to start writing again straight away. Your brain won't handle two modes at the same time.

When I'm writing, the editor side of my brain is forever criticising. 'My god,' it says, 'is that the best you can do? Look at that sentence, it doesn't make any sense; and that metaphor – so cheesy! Come on Gordon, you can't even spell...' and so on. The trick, as the writer Natalie Goldberg points out, is to get to know this editor as intimately as possible: 'the more clearly you know the editor, the better you can ignore it'. Learn to expect what your editor will say, and eventually it'll be like a conversation with your mother-in-law – you'll be able to tune it out.

STRIKING A BALANCE

But, although the writer and the editor may seem like mortal enemies, they need one another in order to make a piece of writing work. Do you remember that episode of *Star Trek* when Kirk and the klingon were trapped together? A balance has to be struck, teamwork has to be nurtured. When inspired, when you feel you simply have to get something down on paper, force the editor in your mind to take a back seat so as not to stop the creative flow. But the next day, when the passion has passed and your creative side has calmed down, let the editor out. Don't be fooled into thinking your creative side has written a perfect piece of writing – trust the editor to read through and make changes.

The internal editor is bound to suggest a few changes – look at IDEA 45, *Surgery or butchery?*, for the best way to handle that red pen.

Try another idea…

PHONE A FRIEND

Don't fall into the trap of being too easily satisfied with your work. Of course you're going to feel an immense amount of pride when you've finished a piece of writing – it's one of the best sensations ever – but don't let this euphoria lead you to a false sense of security. The best way of avoiding this trap is to find a reader you can really trust, somebody not too close to you, but close enough to read through your work regularly. You may feel shy about handing a piece over to somebody, even if you think it's perfect, but the constructive criticism given by a reader will really help you see your work clearly.

Some critics will often impart advice that's spurious, subjective and even downright cruel. And even those critics who are on your side may occasionally offer an honest comment that you're not expecting, that you don't really want to hear. Just remember, when writing you're aiming to let the whole world read, and everybody's got an opinion. If you don't listen to your early critics, you'll have a lot more to deal with later on.

'I have rewritten – often several times – every word I have ever published. My pencils outlast their erasers.'
VLADIMIR NABOKOV

Defining idea…

How did it go?

Q **I don't need to revise the final project because I'm making sure every word is polished to perfection. OK?**

A *Working every word to perfection can stem your creative flow and make your writing seem turgid or false. Rereading is a process best undertaken at the end. And refusing to reread the finished project because you think it will be perfect – well, how cocky is that?*

Q **I've managed to hold back my internal editor for a while but now it's foaming at the mouth in anticipation. I don't want it dissecting the entire piece. What else can I get it to look out for?**

A *It may seem like common sense, but when reading through your work don't ignore the grammar, spelling and punctuation. To have invested so much time, energy and creativity in a piece of writing and then ignore the fine details (yes, I know, the boring fine details) is foolish to say the least, and won't make finding a publisher easy. Use your word processor's spellchecker, but be warned that it won't pick up common errors like 'it's' and 'its'. Read through with a fine-tooth comb simply looking for typos. Or hire a proof-reader or editor – it's often cheaper than you think.*

45

Surgery or butchery?

You'd be surprised how much even the smallest nip and tuck will improve your finished work. Keep your mind open to revision.

The infamous red pen. We've all got one; we all hate to use it. Let's face it: the thought of taking the knife to a piece of writing we've nurtured since birth is tantamount to infanticide.

But rest reassured – this isn't the case. Think of the editing process as more like taking the stabilisers off your kid's bike. It's nerve wracking, and you're worried it will bring them crashing down – but ultimately it makes the ride faster, smoother and a hell of a lot more fun.

CLOSE ENCOUNTERS

When you think your piece is finished, that's when the hard work begins. Working out what to dice and slice from a piece of writing is simply a matter of observation. But what should you be looking for? In short, barnacles and dead wood: anything

Here's an idea for you... **When you've finished your revision, leave it for a day or two and then come back to it. Read through the new version then read through the original. The revised text should be snappier, easier to read and more dramatic. If you cringe a little when rereading your original, great, it just goes to show what a reader's response would have been if you'd sent the work off unedited.**

that's clinging on to the flesh of the piece without contributing anything. You may not think this applies to you, but take a really close look at what you've been writing.

Are there examples of abstractions and generalisations, clichés, outdated or unrealistic language, unwanted or vague description, condescension, didactics, obscurity, poor rhythm or clumsy rhyme, lazy or automatic use of words, stolen phrases you'd meant to change or just plain old waffle? Look at the list above and honestly ask yourself if you're guilty of any of writing's cardinal sins – ask yourself if the piece of writing is unique to you or whether it's something that anybody could have written.

ZOOM LENS

Start by zooming in as close as you can: ask every component of your writing whether it's as well developed as possible, whether it's as good as it can be, and whether it deserves its place in the work as a whole. If it helps, write out sentences separately on a sheet of paper, see if they work as freestanding structures. But don't get so bogged down in detail you forget about the bigger picture – it's vital every now and again to take a step back and look at your finished piece as an organic whole. If you're including everything you've written because you stubbornly don't want to cut it out, you risk a piece of writing full of extraneous detail and devoid of character.

SEEING RED...AND GREEN, AND BLUE

Don't be afraid to let the red pen get carried away. Pare your work down to its purest state, see if it's actually saying what you wanted it to in the first place. Use different coloured pens for comments on plot, or character, or dialogue, so you can get an idea of which area is giving you trouble – if you've got more green marks than any other colour, you know you're having trouble with your dialogue. In fact, you don't even have to limit yourself to a pen. Get messy, attack your draft with scissors and glue, edit the old fashioned way, the messy way – it's so much more satisfying than using a word processor.

Be brave, try major changes like altering the point of view or including a brand new plot twist. It may mean extensive rewriting, but the result may be far more dramatic than your original. The revision period is your chance to try out these changes, so don't be shy. Just never forget to keep a copy of the original. I can't stress this enough. Personal experience has shown me that if you edit on your only copy of a draft, you can never go back, even if you decide the changes you've made suck.

WHOA BOY!

So when is it time to stop revising and leave your work alone? There is no simple answer, but eventually, you'll just know. Like a sculptor chipping away at a block of stone, there will come a point when you don't want to take off any more, when your writing simply speaks for itself. It may take a while for you to recognise it, but believe me, you will.

IDEA 44, *Armageddon*, will show you how to harness your internal editor, so you don't have to leave the pruning till the last minute.

Try another idea...

'The wastebasket is a writer's best friend.'
ISAAC BASHEVIS SINGER

Defining idea...

How did it go?

Q **I can't imagine anything worse than a misinformed surgeon performing a penectomy on a guy who went in for an operation on an ingrown toenail. How do I know if I've made the right cuts and changes?**

A *Ask yourself the following questions of your revised text: are you happy with the finished result? Have you begun in the right place? Do the events of the plot make sense, are they logical or too convoluted? Have you strayed from your theme? Is your research invisible? Can you picture the characters, do they seem realistic and have depth, are their motivations believable and do they talk like real people? Is there conflict, does anything happen? Have you included enough detail to make background and setting believable? Is there a variety of pace? Have you left in any of the 'barnacles' listed above? Are you happy with when you're showing and when you're telling? These are only the basics, but it should get you started, and create chains of thought that lead to other considerations.*

Q **Won't all this revision remove the individuality from my work? Isn't stripping work down bordering on the practice of Newspeak in *Nineteen Eighty-Four?***

A *No. Revision doesn't have to mean getting rid of every detail that makes it personal to you, that makes it your work. On the contrary – you need to be exorcising the repetitions, irrelevancies and badly written phrases that detract from your unique style, that anyone could have written. The fewer weeds growing round the window, the clearer the view will be.*

46

Getting down and dirty

Workshops and writers' groups aren't the terrifying interrogations that the uninitiated often make them out to be. Joining up could be the best thing you've ever done.

Writing can be a lonely profession. Most of the time we sit alone, drinking coffee as we voyeuristically watch other people interacting, or frowning at the blank page muttering to ourselves. Or perhaps that's just me.

Because of this, one of the most severe afflictions to befall a writer is cabin fever, and a resulting inability to see your work objectively. There's only one real cure, and it can seem absolutely terrifying: joining a writers' group.

COME TOGETHER

The thought of showing your work to a group of people, especially fellow writers, can strike fear into the heart of even the toughest of scribes. I remember when I attended my first creative writing meeting my heart was pounding and I was sweating more than a Sumo wrestler in a sauna. But all this stress was unnecessary.

Here's an idea for you... **For academic courses, visit the websites of colleges and universities. Adult education colleges also often offer workshops. Contact your regional arts association for a list of writers' groups in your area open to newcomers or ask local people if they know of any good groups. If all of the above fails, start your own group with any writers you know.**

By the time the meeting settled I understood that each and every person there was in the same boat as me, and equally nervous about the process. The relief of getting to know like-minded writers with the same fears and paranoias as myself was euphoric.

WHY WORKSHOPS?

No writer is truly the best judge of their work. We can't see our writing the way another person would read it, and, as tough as it sounds, we need feedback from other people to make sure it works. Joining a workshop is difficult because it's an admission that perhaps our writing needs improvement. But workshops can make us view our work in a new light, provide us with original ideas and find more powerful ways of saying what we want to say. If you find the right workshop, each session will make you more aware of your potential, more confident in your work; it will give you a better understanding of the process of writing, and of the techniques other people use for success; and it will leave you feeling exhilarated and impatient to write more. Plus, it will inspire you to write: you can't bring your material to a meeting until you've written it.

WHICH WORKSHOPS?

Take your time to find the right environment, and don't be afraid to try more than one group. There is a vast abundance of groups and courses available for writers: ranging from groups who meet informally to postgraduate courses which offer an intensive series of exercises and feedback sessions.

When thinking of joining a group, take the time to work out what you're looking for. Most groups look at several pieces of work a week, usually by different writers, whoever's got something new – the aim being to help a piece

Joining a writers' group can also give you much-needed contacts. See IDEAS 47–51 for information to share with the group.

Try another idea...

of work evolve and grow. Other workshops set exercises to help improve a writer's grip of technique and expression. A good workshop will always feel co-operative not competitive: you are all there to find out how to write successfully, and if you don't work at it as a group you'll all falter.

A DIFFICULT DUTY

Writers' groups demand that you learn to accept constructive criticism – there's no point attending if you don't want to hear other people's opinions. Listen carefully to what people are saying, don't try and argue or contradict, just write it down. Criticism in workshops should always acknowledge the integrity and value of the writing it's aimed at – it shouldn't pick at the flaws, it should point out how the good parts of a piece of writing are weakened by less desirable elements. Criticism should also always be specific – if it's too general, the critic risks giving the impression that it's a writer or his ability to write that is being rejected. Learn to let your work go, to acknowledge the divide between you and your writing, if you want to make the most out of criticism. Be aware that people will interpret your work differently from how you intended, and that this might not necessarily be their fault.

'It's true that writing is a solitary occupation, but you would be surprised at how much companionship a group of imaginary characters can offer when you get to know them.'
ANNE TYLER, US novelist

Defining idea...

205

How did it go?

Q **OK. I'm going to put aside my terror and I'm going to sign up to a writers' group. Are they all as good as each other?**

A *Be warned: not every writing group or course is up to scratch. If you go for the wrong workshop, a single session could leave you feeling ready to throw in the towel completely. Watch out for meetings led by one dominating person, or where members only consider certain forms of writing to be worthwhile; workshops that are competitive and negative, with comments often made about a writer, not their work; and meetings that are too informal, where the criticism is too gentle.*

Q **I do get feedback at workshops, but to be honest I consider my piece finished. It's OK just to ignore the advice, isn't it? Go on, say yes. Please.**

A *There isn't a great deal of point going to a workshop if all you want to hear is 'that's great'. Workshops offer criticism that you should listen to. If you ignore it, your work might never be as good as it could be. Workshops should encourage regular rewriting based around constructive criticism. Try writing your own critique of the piece you're planning to show to the group. Read it as objectively as you can and comment on anything you're not sure about. It won't be easy to see your work in such a negative light, but it will help you respond more constructively to any critical feedback you receive on the night.*

47

Spring cleaning

You wouldn't visit your publisher wearing dirty rags – so don't send them a manuscript that looks like it's just come out of your dog's rear end.

I'm in the rather odd position of being both a writer and a publisher: an internal clash that often threatens to set the two conflicting halves of my personality against one another.

As a writer, when I think I've finished a piece of work I desperately want to send it off straight away, to throw it into the arms of a waiting publisher as it is: naked, raw and screaming. As a publisher, though, I get pretty miffed at people who do just that – who submit their manuscript in an untidy bundle without giving any thought to presentation.

BOG ROLL

That may sound a little harsh, but I'm trying to be as honest as possible. I get anywhere between 20 and 50 submissions a week, from across the board. Most of these are beautifully submitted, but I've had entire novels sent to me unbound and falling all over the place (without the page numbers needed to stack them back in

Here's an idea for you... **Make a template on your word processor now: a title page with your contact details and space for the other information. Also, set up your word processor so that there's always a large margin on the left: it's less to change when you're ready to submit. Don't try typing with double-spacing, though, it can be quite distracting.**

order); poems sent to me on scrap paper and, once, even toilet roll (not used); submissions (badly) handwritten complete with ink stains and margin notes, or so badly laid out on the page that I simply have no idea what's going on.

It's a real shame. These submissions may be masterpieces, but no publisher or editor will devote time to deciphering a poorly presented submission when they could be reading instead. Don't be tempted to experiment with clever presentation tricks in order to woo a publisher or an editor. (I once had half a novel submitted on greaseproof paper – the main character was a chef – the type kept rubbing off on my fingers eventually to the point where I couldn't continue reading.) Avoid annoying a publisher before they've even started reading by following some simple style tips.

KEEP IT CLEAN

Use good-quality A4 paper: it should be clean, white and fairly heavy if it's to survive being thumbed. Leave a large margin on the left hand side (I prefer 4 cm) and space on the other margins: it makes a page much easier and more pleasant to read. Only ever print on one side of the paper (try not to think of the trees). Keep your text clean and well spaced: stick to a size 12 font (black) and always set in double-spacing to avoid a publisher going cross-eyed (we often do when we've been reading submissions all day). Indent the first line of every new paragraph, don't leave extra lines between paragraphs, and always make sure your pages are numbered.

MARK YOUR TERRITORY

Make sure a publisher can see it's your work. On the title page, clearly write your name, address, telephone number, email address and date on the top right-hand side. Write the title of the piece (or a list of poem titles) in the middle of the page, and, at the bottom, write the number of pages submitted and (if prose) the number of words. It's also worth printing your name, telephone number and the title of the submission on the back of every page, so if they get separated from the title page (and believe me they often do) a publisher always knows how to contact you.

FLAT PACKED

Don't fold your manuscript over when sending, or stuff it into a tiny envelope. This is your work, if it doesn't seem like you're proud of it or care about it, then publishers will assume you're not that bothered. Fasten the pages together with a paper clip (or metal paper fasteners if it's a screenplay), not staples. Always include a brief covering letter with your manuscript (and at all costs avoid trying to explain or justify your work – credit publishers with the imagination to work that out by themselves) and a stamped addressed envelope. If a publisher sends the manuscript back and it's a little dog-eared or coffee stained, don't send it out to the next one: print off a new copy. And for God's sake remember to remove any rejection slips a previous publisher has attached before sending it on (it happens more than you'd think).

Honestly, I'm not being anal. These ideas will encourage a publisher to look at your work quickly and favourably. To learn more about sending manuscripts, see IDEAS 48–51.

Try another idea...

'A good many young writers make the mistake of enclosing a stamped, self-addressed envelope, big enough for the manuscript to come back in. This is too much of a temptation to the editor.'
RING LARDNER, US short-story writer

Defining idea...

How did it go?

Q   **OK, I've tidied everything up and I'm ready to submit, but I'm confused by some of the abbreviations publishers use on their guidelines. What's a MSS, a folio and a pp?**

A   *In publishing lingo, MS means manuscript: the hard copy (typescript) of your work. Ignore the etymology of the word: it means a printed copy, not a handwritten one. MSS is the plural; p refers to page, as does folio, and pp means pages.*

Q   **I'm a traditionalist, and my typewriter doesn't have all these new–fangled facilities. Do I have to count up every word myself in order to ensure my word count is exact?**

A   *On the contrary. Never state the exact number of words, always round up or down to the nearest hundred for short fiction or the nearest thousand for full-length books – if a publisher sees 1,358 words, they'll know you're a beginner.*

Q   **Are there any special rules for screenplays?**

A   *If you're sending a screenplay, it's important to remember that each page should represent a fixed time slot. With film, one page equals 1 minute of screen time; with television, 1 page usually represents 30–40 seconds. Use 12 point Courier font with double spacing and you should be spot on.*

48

Learn to let go

The big day has finally arrived. You can't do anything else to your novel – it's perfect. So stop staring at it and get it out there. The world wants to know your name.

As writers, we often like to write for ourselves, but show me a writer who says they don't ever want to be published and I'll show you a fibber.

It's one of the most thrilling experiences imaginable – seeing your own work in print – but the road to success is long and curves in some strange directions, so just remember to brace yourself.

HOME ALONE

The commonest way of approaching a publisher is by going solo. If you're planning to send your novel off there are a few rules you should follow. Don't just send it to the first publisher you come across or the only publisher you know. Do some research, find out which house or imprint is most likely to publish your style or genre – a romance publisher won't accept your horror novel even if it's the best thing they've ever read. Get hold of a publisher's catalogue to see what kind of books they publish.

Here's an idea for you... **Check out a publisher's website, make a note of how many titles they publish and what genres they favour. Are their authors first-timers or seasoned professionals? A little research will ensure you're sending your masterpiece to a publisher who'll treasure it as a product and respect you as an author.**

Alternatively, buy a yearbook that provides information on what a publisher accepts and the guidelines for approaching them.

ON TARGET

Once you've decided which publishers you're aiming for, make sure you follow the correct procedure. When Aztecs approached Montezuma they had to take off their clothes and put on cheap blankets, enter his chamber barefoot and with their eyes cast down, and bow three times saying 'My Lord, my great lord!' If they didn't, they'd get their heads lopped off. Publishers are perhaps a tad less demanding but there are ways of submitting your work without becoming an irritation.

First, don't send in your entire manuscript. Nothing's more likely to get your work sent back unread than an unsolicited novel plopping onto the welcome mat. Instead, write a brief letter to a publisher detailing who you are, and including any information about your past successes and your future plans (publishers like to invest in novelists, so it's always wise to claim you want to make a career of writing, even if you're not sure you do). With this letter, include a 300-word synopsis of your work, and two sample chapters (usually the first two). And never send a proposal to more than one publisher at one time: it's considered very bad form.

A NOT-SO-SECRET AGENT

If going it alone seems too daunting, you might want to think about getting an agent. An agent is somebody who does their utmost to find a publisher for your book, who gets to grips with a contract to make sure you're not getting ripped off, and who incessantly pesters companies to keep publishing your work long into the future. And you get all this for a 10% cut of the earnings from any book they represent. Not bad.

Of course finding a good agent can be just as hard as finding a publisher. If you know somebody with an agent, ask them to recommend you: it's the quickest way to becoming represented. Otherwise, look through a listing of agents (they can be found in writers' yearbooks) and send them a short letter, synopsis and sample chapters. It may seem easier to devote your time to the search for a publisher, but if an agent takes you under their wing your work will be prioritised when it arrives at a publishing house, and you've got a guardian angel who can harass an editor to give you a chance without the risk of making them angry.

A SHORT WORD ABOUT FAILURE

What do *Catch-22, Harry Potter and the Philosopher's Stone, The Time Machine, Sons and Lovers, Moby Dick, The Lord of the Flies, Northanger Abbey, Tess of the D'Urbervilles* and *Animal Farm* have in common? They were all rejected by publishers, often many times. Some famous writers have literally been able to paper their walls with rejection slips. The moral of the story? Never give up, always try, try, try again: every good book will find its home eventually.

Try another idea...

Look at ways to transform your scruffy manuscript into the Cinderella of scripts in IDEA 47, *Spring cleaning.*

Defining idea...

'Curse the blasted, jelly-boned swines, the slimy, the belly-wriggling invertebrates, the miserable sodding rutters, the flaming sods, the sniveling, dribbling, dithering, palsied, pulse-less lot that make up England today. They've got the white of egg in their veins and their spunk is that watery it's a marvel they can breed.'
D. H. LAWRENCE, on hearing that *Sons and Lovers* had been rejected

How did
it go?

Q   **OK, I can't be doing with the rigmarole of approaching publishers. I'd much rather be the master of my own work. So what do you say to vanity publishing?**

A   *Adverts for vanity presses sound too good to be true, and if you send in your manuscript, there are no worries about rejection – it will be accepted straight away. What's the catch? You have to pay for publication yourself. Vanity publishers don't worry about the quality of material they're printing, the only writing they concern themselves with is your signature on a cheque. It's vital to remember that vanity publishers will give you no help with marketing or distribution – possibly the most difficult aspects of publishing to arrange – and repping companies won't always help you out if you're self-published. If your work is good, you shouldn't have to pay to see it in print.*

Q   **Do I have to finish my novel before I approach a publisher? Can't I just send them an idea and write it if they accept? This will save me a whole load of worrying!**

A   *It's extremely unlikely that any publisher will accept a novel before it has been written. Unless you've got a proven track record you need to have written a book before you approach a publisher, even if it's a great, original idea they'll only ask you to come back when it's finished.*

49

Don't cause a drama

Your first script is finished. Great! What are you waiting for? You should whack it straight out to an agent, right? Hold your horses. It's a war out there. Make sure you've got reinforcements.

Many of the big cheeses in film and television production won't take you seriously as a screenwriter until you've got two or three scripts under your belt — showing your depth and variety as a creative thinker and technical writer.

Be patient, when you've finished a script, put it to one side and start another – this commitment to your craft will go a long way to convincing the people who matter. When you've got a couple of ideas, it's time to start hunting. Use your best piece of work as your 'calling card' – the bait to hook a producer or agent. If they like this, they'll ask you if you've got any more. If they sense you're a long-term commitment rather than a one-off they'll be more inclined to bite.

Here's an idea for you... **Make your own filing system: write down the names of producers, agents, production companies and list what projects they've been involved in, what writers they've worked with and any other relevant information. Focus on script development executives, producers, directors and heads of development in film, and look for script editors, commissioning editors, producers and directors in TV. This way, you'll get to know key players and the shape of the industry.**

Script readers pore through hundreds of ideas every year. Your job is to make them look at yours and think 'wow'. In order to do this, you've got to grab their attention in a very short time. When presenting a script, include a tagline: that short slogan that always appears on film posters ('In space, no one can hear you scream'). It has to make your audience want to watch, so make it good. Next comes the one-page synopsis: a single-sided A4 sheet containing a brief, snappy, dynamic outline of the story, the conflict and the target audience. This is your pitch, this is what will get your script accepted or rejected, so make sure you really pull people into the world of your film.

MAKING AN IMPRESSION

Never send out an entire script at once. Instead, write a short letter starting with a little bit about you, saying that you've written a screenplay and stating precisely what kind it is and what genre it's in. At the end of the letter, include a paragraph explaining that you've sent them this information because you think it's a project that might interest them. This letter of enquiry is vital – more so than with any other form of writing. Script readers will assume that if your introductory material is efficient and professional, then your work will be too. Avoid claims such as 'this will be the next eleven-Oscar winner'; they'll think your work isn't good enough to sell itself. Keep it brief and plain – if your idea is good, they'll see it.

IT'S NOT WHAT YOU KNOW...

When trying to break into film or television as a writer it really is about who you know. This is one of the major benefits of getting an agent – they know everybody. If you're going forth without an agent, you've got to start making contacts and working out who's who. Look for producers and production companies in charge of projects similar to your own – watch the credits of films or television programmes, read trade magazines such as *Screen International* or *Broadcast* for information about who's doing what and who's looking for new blood. When you've got names, start phoning and writing. Ask them (or, more likely, their secretaries) if they accept unsolicited manuscripts, and what their submission protocol is.

If you're keen on meeting key players face to face and exercising your networking skills, attend one of the conferences that are held where the speakers are industry executives or writers. Don't be shy, introduce yourself. Try signing up for an extended writing course: these are great places to meet people who can give you a break. You can also join one of the recognised industry bodies, such as Raindance or PACT, where you'll meet plenty of other new writers, producers and directors with whom you can work. For the television writers among you, look at the intern schemes run by independent production companies and TV series. Always remember, whoever you meet, stay polite, courteous and confident without being arrogant.

You can plan your tagline and your pitch when you're plotting your movie – see IDEA 36, *All good things come in threes.*

Try another idea...

'**Roger Corman taught me a very valuable lesson. He said you could make a movie about just about anything as long as it had a hook to hang the advertising on.**'
AMY HOLDEN JONES, screenwriter

Defining idea...

219

How did it go?

Q   Wayhey! I'm ready to submit my script. It's a good 280 pages long but surely that doesn't matter if the quality is good...Right?

A   *Think (at least) twice before submitting this! Make sure your work is the right length for the market. If you're aiming for a feature-length film it shouldn't be longer than 120 pages (remember, 1 minute per page) – and ideally between 90 and 115 pages. Script readers tend to go for the shorter scripts first. It's just as important when writing for TV – always make sure you know the time limitation (including adverts) for the type of programme you're writing for (you can find out by writing or phoning).*

Q   Are the rumours true? Will I have to face a producer and try and sell them my movie face to face? Will they ring a gong if they get bored? Will they release the hounds if I take too long to make my pitch?

A   *One area where screenwriting differs extensively from any other form of writing is the verbal pitch – where you try and directly sell your idea to a big cheese. You can have as little as two minutes to make it work, so you have to have a really strong grasp of characters, their journey, the ending and what kind of people it will appeal to. It's a nerve-wracking thing to have to do, so make sure you know what you're going to say, anticipate any questions, practise and above all show passion for your idea – excitement and enthusiasm are contagious.*

50

The short and curlies

It may be tempting to start sending boxfuls of your poetry and short stories to as many magazines as you can find. But hold up – there are techniques to getting your short work published.

Those of you who write poetry and short stories have it both easier and harder than your novel-writing brethren.

You stand a much greater chance of getting your work published in magazines and multi-author anthologies; but the chances of getting a collection – a book you can call your own – straight away is extremely slim. It's always best to bombard the small magazines before you start sending your work off to Faber & Faber.

CHOOSING CAREFULLY

Knowing which magazine or anthology to submit to is a case of reading as many as possible and getting to know what kind of material each publishes: it's no use sending your short fantasy fiction to a magazine that specialises in Navajo lyrical poetry. Likewise, reading a publication will give you an idea of the quality of the material inside. I've seen some truly dreadful pamphlets that take on pretty much anything submitted to them. If you think the general standard of a magazine is low, you don't really want your work to be associated with it.

Here's an idea for you...

Start looking around for possible outlets for your fiction or poetry. Reference books provide information about most publishers, detailing what kind of material they look for and their terms for submission. Send off for a sample issue, or subscribe to a magazine you feel is particularly suitable for your writing. Getting to know a magazine or journal will give you a much greater understanding of what kind of thing they are looking for, vastly increasing your chances of having work accepted.

It may not seem like it but there are hundreds of literary magazines and anthologies out there. Most are tiny, regional and practically unheard of outside of a small circle of writers, but this doesn't always detract from their quality. If possible, try and find out what kind of distribution a magazine has: does it have a print run of 5,000 distributed nationally or a print run of five passed round the editor's kitchen table? Learn what kind of production values it embraces (whether it's a hastily folded sheet of photocopied A4 or a perfect bound colour journal) and whether it has a good reputation among writers and readers alike.

THE FIRST COLLECTION

Getting your work published in a number of magazines is the best path to take towards your first collection. I won't lie – single-author collections of poetry aren't common, and single-author short story anthologies are even rarer. But this doesn't mean it will never happen. If you're thinking of approaching a publishing house, include a professional-looking pack of material, including a letter explaining that you've got a collection, samples of your published work and any reviews you've been given. Be wary, however, of rushing into publication: make sure you're putting your best work in, otherwise the book reviews you get may make future deals hard to come by. Also, look closely at the companies you approach: some small publishers may be willing to publish your collection but may not have the means, experience or motivation to do a very good job of it. Always look at books they've brought out

previously to get an idea of print and design
quality. It may seem foolish to turn down an
offer of publication, but it might be better in
the long run to wait for a better offer.

**Writing groups can be a source
of information about publishers
and magazines – see IDEA 46,
Get down and dirty, for hints
on finding the right one.**

Try
another
idea...

GOING SOLO

If you're tired of rejection, and want to go it alone, then it is possible to design and
print your own poetry or short story collection. This can be a photocopied
pamphlet or a professionally printed hardback depending on how much you want
to invest. Be very wary when treading this path, however, as the printing is the easy
bit: it's knowing what to do with the mountain of books in your kitchen that's
tricky. It's up to you to generate publicity for your work: contact magazines and
newspapers, send off review copies, attend as many readings and meetings as you
can. The more you're in the public eye, the better your work will sell.

COMPETITIONS

One way to get a head start when looking for
publication is to enter as many writing
competitions as you can find. There are awards
for every type of writing imaginable, some with
pretty impressive prizes including publication
and payment. Winning any award is a major
boost for your own confidence, and may attract
a publishing deal.

*'A modern poet launching
forth his slim volume today is
like a person dropping a
feather over the edge of the
Grand Canyon and then
waiting for the echo.'*
STEPHEN SPENDER

Defining
idea...

225

How did it go?

Q **I'm following your guidelines but fifteen editors in a row have rejected my work. Should I keep putting it down to subjective opinion and try again?**

A *While every editor's choice is subjective, they are all looking for certain criteria when considering submissions. If the same piece of work keeps getting rejected you should ask yourself if it's really your best piece, or if you think it needs a rewrite. Don't change it simply for the sake of pleasing an editor, but do listen to what they're saying – they speak from experience.*

Q **It's taken an editor months to get back to me. Is it rude to send a reminder?**

A *Bear in mind that editors can take two or three months to get back to you about a submission. If you haven't heard back from an editor by the three-month mark, it's perfectly acceptable to send a gentle reminder.*

51

The good, the bad and the ugly

Submitting your work is like dropping your kids off for their first day at school. You don't know whether they are going to be bullied, rejected or become best friends with everybody and make a real impression. Be prepared for all eventualities.

OK, let's defy Wild West tradition and start off with the ugly — and it doesn't get much uglier than this. Rejection.

It's the word that no writer ever wants to hear, but inevitably will at some point in their career. Unless you are extremely lucky, you'll have to learn to cope with rejection. It isn't easy: during the abyss of time between submitting a piece of work and hearing an editor's response you can't help but build up your level of anticipation. And if the response comes back negative it can crush your confidence and make you want to throw everything you've ever written in the fire.

Don't give in. I know it can feel like the end of the world – I used to hide myself away in my room for days on end debating various forms of revenge against the

Here's an idea for you... **It always pays to be careful when you're submitting something for publication. It's rare, but every now and again an editor, publisher or passing janitor might be tempted to pass work off as their own. Print off a copy of the manuscript and all the blurb you've written for it, put it in a sealed, registered envelope and post it to yourself. When you get it back, leave it in a safe place unopened – it can be used as proof that your work was around first.**

offending editor. Put it behind you and try again, with a different editor. Contrary to popular opinion, editors want to open an envelope and be delighted by what's inside, they want to find material worth publishing – they're not out to try and crush your self-confidence by rejecting your work.

TAKE NOTES

Rejection can take many forms. More often than not, you'll get a printed compliments slip with nothing written on it. This is the easiest response for an editor but the most frustrating response for a writer – what did they think? Was it not even worth an acknowledgement? Don't get too wound up, editors are busy and sometimes they simply don't have the time (or are too badly organised!) to respond.

Sometimes the printed slip comes back with some scribbled comments. These might be complimentary: 'good but not quite right for this publication'; promising: 'please send something else'; critical: 'good overall but you haven't quite pinned down the characters'; or just plain derogatory. I won't give an example of the latter, but they do occasionally happen. If you do get a grumpy response, just try to ignore it (the editor's probably got haemorrhoids from sitting down all day) and move on.

PAY ATTENTION

If an editor sees real promise in your work he may take the time to write a more detailed analysis of his decision. Don't take this as an insult and bin the comments, or get on your high horse and write a scathing letter back justifying your work. It's an editor's way of encouraging you to look at certain elements of your writing in order to improve your chances of publication. Take a few days to cool down, then look at what he's saying: it may not be relevant, but he might just be pointing out a weakness you've completely overlooked. Editors don't often make good writers, but they do know what sells and what doesn't. Paying attention to their comments will give you a great advantage next time you submit.

The industry side of writing can be soul-destroying, but try not to get too bogged down in it. Look at IDEA 52, *It's all about you*, for some soothing words.

Try another idea...

AND THE GOOD

If your work runs the gauntlet and makes it from the slush pile, through the juniors or freelancers who'll read it first, and past the senior editor who'll try and sell your book and 'you' the writer to the big cheeses, then you'll get a phone call – quite possibly the best phone call of your life – where an offer is made to publish your book. They might not say this directly, but they will most probably want to meet you to talk about possible changes and to get a feel for how promotable you are as a writer. Once the legal and financial blurb is out of the way, you'll probably have to wait up to eighteen months before you can visit Borders and start drooling over your book on the shelf. It may seem a long wait, but this gives the marketing department time to work their magic and allows the book to be released at the most opportune moment.

'If a publisher declines your manuscript, remember it is merely the decision of one fallible human being, and try another.'
STANLEY UNWIN, publisher

Defining idea...

229

How did it go?

Q **My empty wallet is crying out for nourishment, but I keep hearing people talking about an advance rather than a payment. What's all this about?**

A *The longed-for advance is a lump sum you get based on how much the publisher thinks the book will make on its release. That's all the dosh you'll see unless your percentage of total sales (around 10% of the cover price) reaches the amount you were paid in the advance. If this happens, you get around 10% of every additional copy sold.*

Q **Will I have any say in how my work is produced? Or will it be snatched away from me and brought up by complete strangers?**

A *Depends on the publisher. You'll almost certainly be asked to check proof copies for any typesetting errors. Don't take this moment to rewrite – if you change more than 10% of the original manuscript, you'll probably be asked to pay for typesetting. All good companies will at least consult with you about the cover design, layout and blurb. Don't be afraid to voice your opinion, especially if you're having doubts about something: this is your book, and you're an investment, so publishers will want to keep you happy.*

Q **I'm still paranoid about sneaky little thievses running off with my precious. Any other tips for ensuring copyright?**

A *You can register your work with a solicitor, though this costs. When submitting short stories and articles, you can also write 'First British Serial Rights Offered' (or FBSRO) on the title page, which means you're not prepared to sell copyright.*

52

It's all about you...

If you remember only one thing, make sure it's this: what makes your writing powerful and unique is you, so always learn to trust your instincts.

Creative writing has no real rules; there are guidelines, but ultimately you must write to the beat of your own heart.

LISTEN TO BASHO

The famous Japanese haiku poet Matsuo Bashu gave some wonderful advice on the art of writing: 'Learn the rules; and then forget them.' This doesn't mean go out and whack your head against a wall until you forget everything you've read. It does mean never rely on the guidelines alone to produce a good piece of writing. The ideas are here to help you look into yourself, to help you see the world differently, and to help you learn techniques for giving your work focus and structure. But in order for this advice to translate into powerful fiction, poetry or drama you need to forget about following any set prescriptions and walk your own path. Don't lose sight of what you've learned, but don't get bogged down in it: use it as a way of channelling your energy and creativity on to the page.

Here's an idea for you... **Be courageous. Write about things you're afraid of, things that move you, and be brave enough to try something different – if it doesn't work out, scrap it and try something else. But if it does work you'll end up with something that you will be proud of for years to come. And publishers will beat a path to your door.**

DON'T LET THE BASTARDS GET YOU DOWN

The industry wants you to play by its rules of writing, it wants you to echo its own concept of what the written word should be. But if you really want to make an impact, you have to produce work that means something to you, that resonates with your personality, your beliefs. If you learn to follow Basho's advice, if you learn to use this book to free your creativity, not restrain it, then you will be successful. Indeed, if your writing excites and surprises you, then you're already a success.

PARTING WORDS

The thing to remember, above all, is that even if you're aiming to publish for money, you have to write purely and simply because you love writing. As Wordsworth said, 'fill your paper with the breathings of your heart'. If you focus on getting into print, then what you're writing won't come from the heart, it won't be truly yours. Creative writing must be the most personal of subjects, it must come from your very soul. Write for yourself, write for love, write because you need to discover the truth, because you need to get your heart and soul on paper, because you want to create a world that's all your own, because you don't know what to make of life, because you're afraid, in love, angry; write because you must. Only when you can do this will publishers pay attention. Only when you can do this will your work truly make its mark. Only when you can do this will your work be powerful, and will people love you for it.

Take a good look at IDEA 1, *Limbering up*, and IDEA 2, *Taking the plunge*, and get stuck in!

Try another idea...

'*Everything in life is writable about if you have the outgoing guts to do it, and the imagination to improvise. The worst enemy to creativity is self-doubt.*'
SYLVIA PLATH

Defining idea...

233

How did it go?

Q   I've come down with a bad case of writer's block! Save me!

A   *It's a horrible affliction: sitting at your desk trying to write but not knowing what to say; or knowing what you want to say but for some reason powerless to say it. But writer's block is like the blank page: it seems far worse than it is, and can be beaten with the simplest of scribbles. The block is psychological. I know I've gone on about 'being true to yourself' a great deal in this book, but here's a perfect example why not listening to your inner passions and beliefs can scupper your attempts at writing. If you're not channelling into your emotions, your psychological drives, you've got no energy behind what you write, you've got no oomph. Work out what you're feeling, and why; be honest with yourself, and you should find the blockage shifting.*

Q   And if it still doesn't?

A   *Then you're most likely being too negative about your capacity as a writer. You may be aware of some of your negative thoughts: that perhaps you're not clever or imaginative enough to be a writer; but the chances are a good many of these horrible self-doubts lie deep within your unconscious – perhaps a fear that expressing yourself may lead to ridicule. If you ignore these negative thoughts, or remain unaware of them, they'll pop their ugly heads up again and again. Try and get these thoughts on paper – writing them down in the open, in the light, rids them of their power, makes them look ridiculous. Remember, you're a writer – when your fears exist as words, you've got control.*

The end...

We hope that the ideas in this book will have inspired you to try some new things. You should be well on your way to a more creative, inspired you, brimming with ideas and inventive ambition.

You're mean, you're motivated and you don't care who knows it.

So why not let us know all about it? Tell us how you got on. What did it for you – what helped you beat that blank page with words that fizz? Maybe you've got some tips of your own you want to share (see next page if so). And if you liked this book you may find we have even more brilliant ideas that could change other areas of your life for the better.

You'll find the Infinite Ideas crew waiting for you online at www.infideas.com.

Or if you prefer to write, then send your letters to:
Inspired Creative Writing, The Infinite Ideas Company Ltd,
Belsyre Court, 57 Woodstock Road, Oxford OX2 6JH, United Kingdom

Give us your feedback, let us know which other area of your life needs some improving and you could win a copy of another 52 Brilliant Ideas book. Or maybe you'll decide it's time to tackle a problem and write your own.

Good luck. Be brilliant.

Offer one

CASH IN YOUR IDEAS

We hope you enjoy this book. We hope it inspires, amuses, educates and entertains you. But we don't assume that you're a novice, or that this is the first book that you've bought on the subject. You've got ideas of your own. Maybe our author has missed an idea that you use successfully. If so, why not send it to info@infideas.com, and if we like it we'll post it on our bulletin board. Better still, if your idea makes it into print we'll send you £50 and you'll be fully credited so that everyone knows you've had another Brilliant Idea.

Offer two

HOW COULD YOU REFUSE?

Amazing discounts on bulk quantities of Infinite Ideas books are available to corporations, professional associations and other organizations.

For details call us on:
+44 (0)1865 292045
fax: +44 (0)1865 292001
or e-mail: info@infideas.com

Where it's at...

'Allo 'Allo, 74, 75
abecedaries, 17
abstract, 17, 20–22, 26, 34, 49,
    51–54, 72, 186
academic courses, 204
acceptance of your work, 213–230
adjectives, 17, 49, 50, 142, 189, 191
advance (don't spend it all at once),
    230
adverbs, 48, 49, 50, 112
agents, 215, 218
Animal Farm, 54, 215
anticipation, 77, 168, 198, 227
Arendt, Hannah, 21
Aristotle, 55–56, 159
arts association, regional, 204
Asimov, Isaac, xiii
association, 84, 86, 132, 204
atmosphere, 27, 76, 127, 138
attributive verbs, 70, 72
Atwood, Margaret, 119
Austen, Jane, 92
automatic writing, 38–39

Back to the Future, 115
Banks, Iain, 100
Barthes, Roland, 148
Bashu, Matsuo, 231
believable world, 69
better sex, 1–256
Big Brother, 195
Bishop, Elizabeth, 40
blank page, 1, 2, 4, 52, 203, 234
Bradbury, Malcolm, 97
broadcast, 219
Brown, Dan, 32
Caine, Michael, 89

Calvino, Italo, 101
Campbell, Joseph, 162
Card, Orson Scott, 53
Carver, Raymond, 182
Catch-22, 215
Catcher in the Rye, The, 55
character(s), xiv, 4, 6, 11–14, 18,
    26–27, 30–32, 34, 46, 52–62,
    65–69, 71–80, 83–100, 102,
    106–112, 114–117, 119,
    123–126, 128, 131–134, 141,
    146–147, 149–155, 160–162,
    164–173, 181–184, 186–187,
    190–192, 196, 200–202, 205,
    210, 220, 228
character-driven narrative, 56
Chekhov, Anton, 187
chin, taking it on the, *see* feedback
chronology, 156
circles, speaking in, *see* circumlocution
circumlocution, 48
    see also speaking in circles
classical narrative structure, 150
clichés, 44, 52, 143, 200
climactic event, 160–161
climax, 153, 155, 160–162, 167, 170,
    173–174
Clockwork Orange, A, 76
competitions, 184, 225
conflict, 2, 77–80, 88, 110, 154–155,
    170, 182–183, 202, 218
copyright, 230
Corman, Roger, 219
critical choices, 154, 155
cummings, e. e., 45
Cunningham, Michael, 98

Da Vinci Code, The, 32, 166
Davis, Miles, 15
daydreaming, 31
de Beauvoir, Simone, 118–119
De Vries, Peter, 191
detail, 4, 11–14, 18, 26–27, 58–59,
    125–126, 128, 134, 136–137,
    141–142, 151, 187, 200, 202
developing characters, 150
dialect, 73, 74, 76, 98
dialogue, 69, 70–72, 75–76, 93, 106,
    160, 189, 196, 201
Dickens, Charles, 91
Doctor Who, 117, 127
Doctorow, E. L., 61
dreams, 7, 16, 107, 138, 169
Dryden, John, 67
Duffy, Carol Ann, 40

editing, 70, 94, 136, 156, 191, 195,
    199
Egg Box, The, 136
electrocardiograms (monitoring your
    plot), 164, 166
Eliot, George, 92
Eliot, T. S., 21
Emma, 55
emotion, 7, 21–22, 39, 51–52, 96,
    102, 186
English language, 47, 49
exercises, 15, 36, 46, 50, 68, 96, 98,
    102, 108, 118, 120, 126,204,
    205
experimenting, 108, 118, 182
expressing yourself, 234
exquisite corpse, 16–17
    see also exercises

feedback, 204, 206, 236
Fighting Fantasy, 99, 101
final goal, 161
first person, 75, 96–98, 101,
   105–110, 115, 118, 125
Fitzgerald, F. Scott, 57
flashbacks, 26, 72, 114–116
Flaubert, Gustave, 45
Ford, Ford Madox, 173
Forster, E. M., 55–56, 58, 111,
   149–150
Fowler, Gene, 3
Fowles, John, 110
Frost, Robert, 39, 85

games, 7, 15–18
generalisation, 22
Gielgud, John, 123
Goldberg, Natalie, 196
Good Will Hunting, 160
Gordimer, Nadine, 183
grammar, 114, 116, 198
Great Expectations, 55
Great Gatsby, The, 55, 109
Greene, Graham, 192
Grigson, Geoffrey, 35

Hamlet, 155
handbooks, for writers, 214–215
Harry Potter, 55, 215
Heart of Darkness, 106
Hemmingway, Ernest, 191
Herdman, Ramona, 40
Hubbard, Elbert, 13

iambic pentameter, 33–34
imagery, 54, 144
imitating, 39
initiating event, 153–155, 160, 164,
   166
interior monologue, 102, 106, 115
irony, 93
Ishiguro, Kazuo, 152

James, Henry, 57, 97
Jones, Amy Holden, 219
Joyce, James, 97

Karp, Vickie, 155
Konner, Lawrence, 169

language, 30, 34–35, 38–39, 44–45,
   47–49, 51, 54, 74, 76, 131, 144,
   177, 200
Lardner, Ring, 211
Larkin, Philip, 39
Lawrence, D. H., 125, 215
Lawson, Doug, 79
Le Guin, Ursula K., 151
line breaks, 34, 36
local writers, 135, 138
Lodge, David, 93, 120
Lord of the Flies, The, 215
Lord of the Rings, The, 76, 163

Madame Bovary, 80
Mansfield, Katherine, 182
manuscripts, presenting, 209–212
markets, seeking, 184, 220
masterpieces, 210
Maugham, W. Somerset, xiii
memories, 4, 14, 22, 25–28, 38, 39,
   52, 137, 142
Men's Health, xiv
metaphor, 14, 21–22, 47, 52–54,
   142–144, 192, 196
metre, 33–35
Milligan, Spike, 129
Milton, John, 34
Moby Dick, 215
models in poetry, 39
Mona Lisa, 11
Montezuma, 214
muse, 5, 7, 15–16

Nabokov, Vladimir, 197
narrative, 49, 51, 56–57, 66, 75, 91,
   94–95, 99–100, 102, 105–106,
   110–111, 115–120, 125, 150,
   155, 166, 174, 181, 188
needless repetition, *see* repetition,
   needless
Nin, Anaïs, 133
Nineteen Eighty-Four, 202
non-human narrators, 108
Northanger Abbey, 215
notebooks, 6, 136

O'Connor, Flannery, 27, 138
objective correlative, 21–22
Officer Crabtree, 75
omniscient third person, 92, 96
Onetti, Juan Carlos, xiv
Orwell, George, 54, 147

pacing, 36, 162, 168
PACT, 219
pathetic fallacy, 133
Peck, John, 143
people watching, 6
Peoples, David Webb, 161
personal experience, 188
Petrarchan sonnet, 178
Picasso, Pablo, 66
Pierre, D. B. C., 101
Plath, Sylvia, 233
plot, xiv, 6, 27, 30, 55–58, 67, 70, 78,
   80, 87, 93, 117, 145–156, 159,
   160, 162, 164–167, 171–174,
   182–183, 187, 190, 196,
   201–202
plot-driven narrative, 56
plotting, 117, 119, 150–152,
   154–155, 159, 162–163,
   168–169, 219
Poe, Edgar Allan, 18, 182
poetry, 14, 16–17, 19, 20, 30, 33–40,
   43, 45–46, 65, 102, 116, 142,
   177–180, 185–186, 223–225,
   231

presenting manuscripts, 209–212
Procrustes, 184
prose, 14, 20, 30, 34, 36–37, 43, 50,
    65, 100, 102, 116, 166,
    185–186, 211
Proust, Marcel, 25
publishing, 212, 215–216, 224–225,
    228

qualifiers, 48, 50

Raindance, 219
Reade, Charles, 165
rejection, 211, 215–216, 225, 227
repetition, needless, *see* tautology
rereading, 190, 200
research, 30–32, 44, 79, 128–129,
    202, 213–214
resistance (is not useless), 155, 170
rhyme, xiv, 177–180, 200
rhythm, xiv, 33–37, 39, 179, 192, 200
rules, xiii, 30, 36, 66, 72, 109, 113,
    116, 119, 153, 171, 212–213,
    231, 232

Screen International, 219
screenplays, 2, 5, 77, 88, 113, 141,
    146, 159–162, 167–169, 171,
    173, 211–212, 218
second person, 17, 99, 100–102
seeing things in a new light, 11–14,
    204
self-publishing, 216
senses, 20, 26–27, 52, 136, 186
sentimentality, 22
setting, xiv, 26, 31, 76, 89, 123,
    125–130, 134, 141–142, 164,
    187, 202
settings, 31
sex, better, see better sex
Shakespeare, William, 34
Shaw, George Bernard, 137

short stories, 136, 181–184, 223, 230
show (don't tell), 15, 21, 25, 62, 77,
    86, 90, 111, 112, 150, 161, 165,
    170, 185, 186–188, 200–201,
    206, 213, 220
Singer, Isaac Bashevis, 201
soap operas, 62
Sons and Lovers, 215
Sophie's Choice, 154
speaking in circles, *see* circles,
    speaking in
speech registers, 44–45
Spender, Stephen, 225
Star Trek, 196
Star Wars, 162
Steinbeck, John, 129
Stevenson, Robert Louis, 125
stream of consciousness, 66
structure, 34, 38–39, 89, 118, 150,
    153, 156, 159–160, 162, 169,
    179–180, 184, 231
style, xiv, 29, 43–46, 71, 75, 92,
    94–95, 98–99, 102, 106, 110,
    115, 117–120, 159, 166, 202,
    210, 213
subjects, 2, 19, 20, 233
submitting screenplays, 217–220
submitting work, 209–212
subplots, 171– 174
support characters, 90
surprises, 16, 151, 154–155, 190, 232
suspense, 136, 147, 151, 164, 166,
    168–169, 170, 183
Swift, Graham, 110
Swordfish, 160
symbols and symbolism, 21–22, 52,
    54, 134, 141, 143–144
sympathy, 61, 89

tautology, 49
tense, 113–119, 165
Tess of the D'Urbervilles, 215

theme, 39, 95, 97, 118, 145–148,
    172–174, 178, 202
third-person limited, 95–96, 98, 125
three-act structure, 159–162
Time Machine, The, 215
Tolkien, J. R. R., 76
Tolstoy, Leo, 145
transformation, 147
Trollope, Anthony, 71
Twain, Mark, 108
Twain, Mark, 49, 179
Tyler, Anne, 205

Unwin, Stanley, 229
Updike, John, 17
using models, 39–40, 62

vanity publishers, 216
verbal pitch, 220
viewers, engaging, 170
virtual shifts, 112
vocabulary, 14

Waiting for Godot, 123
Wells, H. G., 189
Welsh, Irvine, 74
Welty, Eudora, 31
Westlife, 22
White, E. B., 50
Wilde, Oscar, 7, 107
Williams, William Carlos, 17
Woolf, Virginia, 4, 97
Wordsworth, William, 26, 34, 233
workshops, 185, 204–206
writer's block, 234
writers' groups, 203–206
Wuthering Heights, 133

Yeats, W. B., 38–40, 44